The God Who Doesn't Exist

Fergus McGinley

The God Who Doesn't Exist

God In An Evolutionary World

Fergus McGinley

Adelaide
2025

Text copyright © 2025 remains with the Fergus McGinley. All rights reserved. Except for any fair dealing permitted under the Copyright Act, no part of the publication may be reproduced by any means without prior permission. Inquiries should be made in the first instance with the publisher.

A Forum for Theology in the World
Volume 12, Issue 1, 2025

A Forum for Theology in the World is an academic refereed journal aimed at engaging with issues in the contemporary world, a world which is pluralist and ecumenical in nature. The journal reflects this pluralism and ecumenism. Each edition is theme specific and has its own editor responsible for the production. The journal aims to elicit and encourage dialogue on topics and issues in contemporary society and within a variety of religious traditions. The Editor in Chief welcomes submissions of manuscripts, collections of articles, for review from individuals or institutions, which may be from seminars or conferences or written specifically for the journal. An internal peer review is expected before submitting the manuscript. It is the expectation of the publisher that, once a manuscript has been accepted for publication, it will be submitted according to the house style to be found at the back of this volume.

All submissions to the Editor in Chief are to be sent to: hdregan@atf.org.au.

Each edition is available as a journal subscription, or as a book in print, pdf or epub, through the ATF Press web site—www.atfpress.com. Journal subscriptions are also available through EBSCO and other library suppliers.

Editor in Chief
Hilary Regan, ATF Press

A Forum for Theology in the World is published by ATF Theology and imprint of ATF (Australia) Ltd (ABN 90 116 359 963) and
is published twice or three times a year.

ISBN: 978-1-923206-94-6 soft
       978-1-923206-95-3 hard
       978-1-923206-96-0 epub
       978-1-923206-97-7 pdf

Published by

THEOLOGY

Making a lasting impact

An imprint of the ATF Press Publishing Group
owned by ATF (Australia) Ltd.
PO Box 234
Brompton, SA 5007
Australia
ABN 90 116 359 963
www.atfpress.com
Making a lasting impact

A Forum for Theology in the World Vol 12 No 1/2025

Table of Contents

Introduction		vii
1.	Deus ex Machina	1
2.	The Career of the Gods	13
3.	A Living Universe	33
4.	What's so Original about Sin?	51
5.	No Plan B	77
6.	Messiah Complex	91
7.	The Church and the Counterfeit Gospel	113
8.	The Gospel Strikes Back	129
9.	Reality Itself	143
Bibliography		165

A Forum for Theology in the World Vol 12 No 1/2025

The God Who Doesn't Exist

'Kill some more, steal some more.'

'Pyotr Stepanovich is handin' me that same advice, in them same words as you, 'cause he's a real stingy and hard-hearted man when it comes to givin' assistance. Besides which, he ain't got no belief at all in the heavenly creator, who fashioned us out o' the dust of the earth. He says it's jes' nature made everythin', even down to the last animal, and besides, he ain't got no understandin' that the likes of us jes' can't get along unless we get some beneficial assistance. You start tryin' to explain to him, he stares at you like a sheep at the water, you can't do nothin' but marvel at him.'

[Fedya the convict to Stavrogin in Demons by
Dostoevsky, 1871–1872, Chapter 2[1]]

Introduction

It is 2024, late in the year, as I write. The world is facing a remarkable conjunction, a veritable 'polycrisis'.[2] On one hand, global events which seem to present an existential threat to humanity: the continuing

---

1. Fyodor Dostoevsky, *Demons* [1871–1872], English translation by RA Maguire (London: Penguin, 2008).
2. An expression first used by French complexity theorists Edgar Morin and Anne Brigitte Kern in their 1999 book *Homeland Earth* (New York, Hampton Press), now the buzz word of the moment: 'As the world navigates the polycrisis—climate change, pandemic, the war in Ukraine, economic slowdown, inflation, food insecurity, monetary tightening and debt distress—we need multilateral cooperation and solidarity now more than ever.' WTO Director-General Ngozi Okonjo-Iweala, *Weekend Australian*, 24–25 December 2022.

climate crisis, the Russian invasion of Ukraine grinding on into a third year with the real threat of nuclear conflict, the powder keg of Israel/Palestine suddenly exploding, global economic disruption, social and political polarization in the west, threats to democracy with the rise of authoritarianism and the uncontrolled development of AI, the continuing fear of rogue viruses and pandemic. Help! On the other hand, a situation which has developed with increasing rapidity over the last hundred years or so in which, for the first time in human history, a very large group of people, the majority in the global west, have ceased believing in God.

You are probably not so worried about the second thing, the rise to cultural dominance in the west of atheism, I would hazard to guess—does it really matter what people believe in the abstract, when you have a concrete situation of such dire proportions facing you? But I think you should be, or should at least hear alarm bells going off in your head, because the apparent departure of God leaves us existentially alone in the world, to fend for ourselves and solve our own problems, just when we're facing the first thing, challenges of a global nature which threaten our very existence. We are the ones who have got ourselves into this pickle in the first place, courtesy of a whole lot of thoughtless, careless, self-serving behaviour, on behalf of most or even all of us, over a long period of time, and now we imagine we can save ourselves with no outside help?!

Hang on, I thought all these problems were caused by other people or other things, not me—greedy capitalists, for example, the ruling classes, the patriarchy, the 'system'? Yes, fearful systemic, collective, cultural forces have developed over the long timespan of human history, forces whose real power and intentionality can only truly be captured by the term 'evil', which are far beyond the best possible efforts of mere individuals to combat. It is these forces that right now seem to be conspiring to bring about our polycrisis. No wonder we're all so freaked out!

But no, the origin of even the most powerful cultural evil is always in individual selfishness and self-seeking—or do we imagine real devils and demons out there, or perhaps aliens, luridly grinning, mocking us, conducting the mayhem?! You and me, in other words: we are all complicit. It is *my* inner narcissist, therefore, my inner racist, materialist, sexist, bigot, that needs dealing with first—my natural-born self-centred self. Best of luck with that, however: it is beyond the power of any one of us to change even just ourselves deep down inside, let alone the collective of the entire human race!

Welcome, then, to *The God who doesn't exist*—the God we created ourselves long ago, unwittingly perhaps, believed in just about forever, then only very recently dumped. It was a God we tried so hard to inveigle into saving us, which never really worked, because all along we had the wrong idea of what we needed saving from! Fortunately, however, it turns out that God does exist, as we will unfold in this book—a different one to the one who doesn't exist, obviously!

The God who exists: if you hang on to your hats, we are going to attempt some *anti-theology*, conventional theology in reverse. Thus, rather than starting by assuming God exists when they clearly do not, then vainly trying to work out what they are like, we are going to work in reverse: start from the obvious fact of God's non-existence, then attempt to show that God must, nevertheless, actually exist. An ambitious, if confusing project, I'm sure you will agree!

There will be some *anti-science* too, because, like theology, modern science also starts by assuming too much. We will attempt to get behind the prevailing scientific assumption that the universe is purely physical, a view of the world that, far more than the proclamations of the great ones like Marx, Nietzsche, Freud, Dawkins and Hitchens, has sounded the death knell of God in the modern era. Like the God who doesn't exist, we will see that the purely physical universe is a human fabrication, amazingly useful when it comes to solving the world's practical problems and developing marvellous technology, but not a universe in which there is any place for a God who exists.

Anti-theology and anti-science: the task of the first three chapters. As we will see, God's real existence is the only possible explanation for the one and only human capacity that will enable us to dig ourselves out of the current hole we are in, namely the capacity to be, contrary to our nature, considerate, respectful, caring of each other—the capacity, dare I say it, to practice, at least some of the time if not a lot of the time, a little selflessness or selfless love. A capacity, by the way, which is the only thing that has prevented us, *homo sapiens*, from tearing ourselves to bits long ago, and, for that matter, has enabled us to do anything good with our (human) lives at all, ever.

My argument will be that selflessness, practised by humans, exists in the world, there is plenty of it around in fact, perhaps increasingly so as time goes on—even if right now we could do with an extra blast of it to get us through our present trials—but it doesn't and cannot come, naturally, from inside of us, so it must have come from the outside. Therefore, ipso facto, QED, there must be a selfless love source outside humanity; and that, of course—an amazing, radical hypothesis—is none other than the central character of this book, the God who doesn't exist!

Oops, no, I mean the God who exists—obviously! A situation has developed in human history which would be hilarious if it wasn't the source of virtually all our ills: two Gods in parallel, continually at cross-purposes, a real one we didn't create and a fake one we did. You can see this in the famous Garden story from the Hebrew Old Testament which we will get to by Chapter 4—a story which has its counterparts in many other religious traditions around the globe—with the real God, who has nothing but good things in store for his creatures, at odds with the first humans who imagine they can be mighty gods themselves—but don't take it literally, whatever you do!

Another place to see it is in the New Testament Gospel stories, with the disciples continually mistaking what sort of Messiah Jesus would be, what sort of Kingdom he would inaugurate. Jesus, in fact, was the bearer of the original Messiah complex, as we will see in Chapter 6. We'll make the outrageous claim that he was the unique, literal incarnation into the world of the real God, precisely in order to put the fake God to the sword, and, yes, proclaim a real Kingdom, very different to the one everybody was expecting, and which we're all in now 2000 years later.

Eek!—yes, completely outrageous, because, clearly, I am now daring to follow one particular religious tradition to the exclusion of all others. That won't actually be the case however, because we will realise that Jesus came to set us free from all religion, all human cultural structures that bind people up, with the God who doesn't exist his chief target. The irony is that, contrary to his intentions—another controversial claim—Jesus' followers, almost from the moment he, as the story goes, ascended back up to heaven, set about creating a new religion of their own, complete with what is now a social mega-institution, the Christian Church.

Vent your fury on the Church, and Christianity, by all means—for inventing a counterfeit Gospel, a fake version of the good news of the Kingdom Jesus came to inaugurate, setting itself up as the gatekeeper of a different kingdom, a heavenly one beyond this mortal coil, at the same time as allying itself with the very social and cultural hegemonies Jesus' Kingdom was intended to sweep away. The reality of it is, as we'll see in Chapters 7 and 8, that only in spite of itself has the Church done any good in the world, made any headway at all in fulfilling its Jesus-given task of being what I call a 'pilot-project' of the Kingdom.

Great headway has indeed been made in the last 2000 years—but now we are mired in the polycrisis and still mistaking the God who doesn't exist for the one who does. So, what exactly is this 'Kingdom' that I have now referred to five times without explaining? Well, Jesus himself referred to it around a hundred times without explaining, so why should I?! The problem is not in the explaining, anyway, but in the getting. It is defined as much by what it is not as by what it is—as you will see in what follows.

The Kingdom is nothing more, as it turns out, than an objective state of human relationships in the world based on selfless cooperation, inclusive of all people everywhere, all the time—and if that sounds to you suspiciously like the ideal of (dare I say it) democracy, you would be right. No, not a theocracy: the God whom we thought didn't exist is not that sort of God! What binds the people together in this Elysian ideal is not an abstract, secular ideal of equality, but faith in an invisible God of love. A commonwealth, a republic of God if you like.

Faith in an invisible God of love: only through such faith, through no personal effort of our own, can the 'great turning', the *metanoia*, the radical inner transformation from natural selfishness to very unnatural selflessness, occur—for any one of us, for the entire human race to just survive, let alone thrive. This is the particular Kingdom that is always coming, the one Jesus of Nazareth spoke of incessantly all those years ago—even if things right now seem to be going decidedly in the reverse direction in these polycrisis days.

This will be an evolutionary tale, and we will follow three stories entwined. First, the evolution of our own species, *homo sapiens*, gradually emerging out of a background of precursor primate and hominid species, cursed seemingly with a radically new trait, self-consciousness, perhaps the real source of all our woes. Second, the gradual unfolding of God's (the one who exists') so-called 'plan of salvation' for this woebegone new creature. Third, the development of individual humans, you and me, from childhood to maturity, with our parents acting, critically, *in loco dei*, in the place of God—but make sure you channel the right God, whatever you do!

It is also my own story, by the way, nearly seven decades now of confusion and self-doubt, with perhaps some small degree of clarity only very recently emerging—but I won't bore you with that . . . Ah, false modesty, you're immediately thinking, to conceal the true offensiveness of his thesis: one place, one time, one man, to the exclusion of all others—you just can not come at it, no matter how nicely he dresses this God of love up. The man Jesus himself might have been staunchly anti-colonialist, murdered as he was by Imperial Rome, and certainly he always was on the side of the poor, the sick, the marginalized ones; but his later followers marched arm in arm with the European colonial invaders who brought so much misery and dispossession to indigenous peoples the world over. Then there is the whole notion of resurrection from the dead, eternal life, defying common sense and the scientific laws of nature we so revere—no, a thousand times, no, you swear! Yes, you will have plenty of opportunities throughout my tale to voice your concerns, to shout at me even, please be assured. But now, if you dare, suspend your disbelief, and read on.

A Forum for Theology in the World Vol 12 No 1/2025

Chapter 1
Deus ex Machina

You and I—*homo sapiens*—are now thought to have been around for about 300,000 years, having evolved from various earlier hominid species over maybe a million years. We have not just survived—against the elements, against competition with other species and with each other—but thrived, making us right now, in the early twenty-first century, the unrivalled super species of the planet. We dominate land, water and air, and far from threatening us, many other living species, animal and plant, are in serious danger of being made extinct by our activity. A key aspect of our ability to survive and thrive and achieve such dominance, the real secret of it in fact, has been our capacity to develop ways of living together cooperatively, not just on a small scale, in small family and community groups, but also on an increasingly larger scale, in tribes, societies, nations, eventually, now, globally. In fact, evidence has recently been emerging that homo sapiens won the evolutionary race over other early hominid species such as neanderthals, precisely because of its apparent ability to form larger, more inter-dependent and resilient social groupings.[1]

You might be surprised to hear this, given the problems of human cooperation we rehearsed in the introduction, the polycrisis the world now faces! But living cooperatively together has always been both our great opportunity and our great challenge. It is an opportunity, for the obvious reason that successful cooperation turbo-charges our prospects of survival. But it is also a challenge because cooperation doesn't come naturally to us—we are not like ants and bees, those paragons of organic cooperation, whose body parts and instincts

---

1. See, for example, Kate Ravilious, *Survival of the friendliest? Why Homo sapiens outlived other humans*, in *New Scientist*, 24/11/21.

are purpose-adapted for the task—so we have had to learn the art of conscious, intentional cooperation. And to cooperate fruitfully in the long term—to grasp the opportunity and not just survive but thrive—we have needed to acquire, somewhere along the line, in some degree and to some extent, a capacity, as we described it in the introduction, for selflessness, for selfless love. Selflessness—or 'altruism', as it is referred to in biology and philosophy—is the X-factor without which human cooperation can never really get past square one.

Our nature is the problem. You can see this clearly any day of the week by observing little children when they first emerge into the world and set out learning the ropes of life. We humans are born neither innately good nor bad, but innately self-centred, self-absorbed. How could it be otherwise? A human child, when it is first born, lives and acts in a purely unconscious, direct experience of itself, neither selfish nor selfless, just a consciousness absorbed in itself, not yet awakened to the reality of the world outside. Initially, this is not in any way a negative quality—not what we might call 'original sin', for example—rather, just a simple, default fact of our nature.

Why is this a problem? Well, I am sure you will agree that the innocent, self-absorbed behaviour of little babies and children can be very charming and affecting, but as they grow this can turn into a wilfulness that is very challenging and problematic for their parents and, later, others to deal with. What is emerging in the child is the uniquely human capacity of self-consciousness. We'll have a lot more to say about this interesting little human trick in subsequent chapters, and while it is certainly true that some non-human animals exhibit self-consciousness to a limited degree, we humans seem to specialize in it. As we will see, conscious awareness of self as a distinct self is simultaneously also consciousness of others as selves, but initially the child only cares about one particular self, namely itself. Why should it care about anyone else? Why should any of us ever care about anyone else, for that matter? Caring about yourself is natural and self-evident in life, but caring about others is downright unnatural, far from an obvious thing to do.

Initially in a child's life, therefore, others—principally parents, obviously—seem to be there only to give it what it wants, play with it as directed, cater for its every whim. This sounds charming and idyllic, but it doesn't last; very quickly, inevitably, the self-centred wants of the child bump into the needs, wants and limitations of others, and the urgent necessity for the child to start learning what is completely unnatural—some knowledge and skill in cooperating with others—cuts in. What now begins is the crucial, central task of parenting: to not just provide for the physical needs of the child, but to also teach it how to live cooperatively in the world with others. Gradually other parties join in the great task—extended family, teachers, eventually community, society at large. All the pathologies of human behaviour—everything from children not playing nicely together in the playground, to the types of selfish behaviour that lead to global conflict and environmental crisis—have their ultimate roots in the inadequacies, limitations and failures of this vital human task of parenting and preparing a child for the adult world.

Cooperative behaviour: teaching the child, yes, to play nicely, to consider others, to smile, to be polite (say hello, please and thank you, answer questions sensibly), to say sorry and to forgive, to be kind, generous, thoughtful, helpful, to be prepared to sometimes put the needs and desires of others before their own needs and desires, and so on. All these things, without exception, at their root, require some real non-zero modicum of genuine selflessness, of selfless love. The one certainty is that the child will never work out how to do any of these things by itself, without the help of parents and others, so that if the child is merely left to its own devices, or the parents botch the process badly and no one in the community around comes to the rescue, it will never 'grow up', and in adult life will almost certainly become an uncooperative, selfish, dysfunctional, plain bad person— who might achieve some temporary success as a megalomaniac, a criminal, or a psychopath, but will more likely just live an isolated, miserable and probably short life.

Selflessness, selfless love: the capacity to, even if just for an instant, let go of our own self-interest in favour of the interest of another. Only a self-conscious creature is capable of pulling off such a feat— you cannot let go of yourself if you have no awareness of yourself as a self; there's nothing to let go of—and even then it's the last thing we are naturally inclined to do. This type of love, the essential ingredient of even the simplest little act of consideration, respect or kindness, is different in kind, not just degree, to all the other things we commonly call love, natural human loves such as the love of one's lover, family, friends, sporting team or country. The classical Greek word for selfless love is *agape*, in contrast to human loves such as *eros* (romantic love), *philia* (friendship love) and *storge* (family love). In English *agape* is sometimes characterized as 'love for everyone' or 'universal love', as if it was merely an expanded, extrapolated form of natural human love; but, as we will see, no amount of expanding or extrapolating human love can bridge the difference in kind between the two. Selfless love is unconditional, open, inclusive, not looking for or expecting anything in return, in contrast to human loves, which are closed, conditional and exclusive, limited to particular individuals or groups that are the objects of our love—even if we self-deceivingly imagine we have big enough a heart to somehow love everyone and everything.[2]

I promise you we will keep hammering home this point: selfless love is not natural, it is a different species or kind to natural human loves. And it's precisely because selfless love does not come naturally to a human child that parents have no choice but to teach it. How do we pull off that little miracle? In the beginning, and most essentially, by practising and modelling it ourselves: we smother our little darlings with every ounce of love, of gentleness, kindness, affection, care, we can summon up. We smile at them, sing to them, kiss them, cater for every physical and emotional need we imagine they might have; it is a no holds barred, unconditional, love offensive.

What happens when the opposite occurs, however: parents and society completely withhold love and care from a child? You may never have thought about this question before because it hardly bears thinking about. Child neglect and abuse are really the worst of human tragedies, inflicting long term, often generational damage on individuals, families, communities and societies. Parents and immediate communities are not always primarily to blame either—witness the terrible impact of violent conflict, forced migration, colonisation, both historically and in the present day, in preventing parents from being able to bring up their children in the best possible way, or even at all (in the case of children being orphaned).

Obviously, no one will ever perform a controlled scientific experiment to confirm that this claim is true—that development of the capacity for selfless love in humans is absolutely dependent on

---

2. Some recommended further reading on this topic: Henri Bergson, *The Two Sources of Morality and Religion* [1932], English translation by RA Audra and C Brereton (London: Macmillan, 1935); CS Lewis, *The Four Loves* [1960] (London: William Collins, 2012); Alexandre Lefebvre, *Human Rights as a Way of Life* (Stanford: Stanford University Press, 2013).

positive outside intervention from other humans who have already acquired the capacity—but I think it is a pretty safe extrapolation from the uncontrolled evidence at hand. Consider, for example, evidence emerging from Romania after the fall of the dictator Ceaușescu in 1989, where thousands of children had been abandoned in orphanages and brought up with little or no basic human contact, leading to severe physical, emotional and social delays.[3]

The good news, however, once you get over terrible thoughts about the vulnerability of little children and the dire consequences of neglect and abuse, is that generally the process works pretty well, and most children grow up with a reasonable capacity for selflessness and are therefore able to participate positively in family, community and society. But the selfless love has to be the genuine article and unless there is some of it somewhere in the mix, the whole thing will collapse like a house of cards. The human cooperation game is about being able to build sustainable and fruitful alliances with others, through play, friendship, sport, creative activity, work, family and so on, and people sooner or later see through and spurn someone who is just faking it—someone who might just be going through the motions of genuine consideration of others, when they are really only interested in what they can get out of people for themselves.

It is completely unnatural—genuine selflessness—even if most of us seem to take to it readily and naturally, and even if it becomes, in some or even many of us, what appears to be a natural, lifelong habit. For the obvious reason that it requires us to do something that goes against our entire evolutionary upbringing: let go of our innate drive to survive purely on our own account for a moment, and place another's survival and wellbeing first. Let go of self: something that it never occurred to life to do till we came along!

You probably smell some species exceptionalism here, which we will certainly come back to later and interrogate more. But, as I have said, it is more by way of opportunity/challenge than thinking we're better than the rest. We cannot help how nature has made us: minimal instincts to get us past even survival square one on our own, but with an over-sized brain so that we have an unparalleled ability to learn new

---

3. See, for example, Wikipedia, *1980s-1990s Romanian orphans phenomenon* at <https://en.wikipedia.org/wiki/Romanian_orphans>. Accessed 18 November 2024.

tricks. A central part of the opportunity/challenge, beyond (mere) big brains, is, as we have already mentioned, and postponed a detailed discussion of till Chapter 4, our capacity for self-consciousness. It makes us the first ever full-blown egomaniacs, but at the same time furnishes us with the key to the way out of that egotism by learning selflessness, namely some sense of what it is actually like to be a self ourselves.

At any rate, my hypothesis, as you can probably tell, is that no human child ever learns the capacity for selflessness, so essential for successful cooperative behaviour, without outside intervention—by other, pre-existing human beings (parents, principally, then others in community and society around them) who have already previously, presumably, learned something of the art of selfless love themselves. Thus, in the normal scheme of things, parents teach their children to be selfless on the basis of the selflessness they have learned from their parents, who in turn learned it from their parents—and so on, presumably, back down through the generations. This simple, rather innocuous-looking hypothesis immediately throws up an amazing question, however: if no human ever learns, or has ever learned, to love selflessly without outside intervention, who or what is there outside humanity that could have started the love ball rolling in the first place?

The answer is God, of course—at least that's how, as we will see, human beings have understood it throughout most of history, right until very recently—a God who must really exist 'out there' somewhere, outside of and independently of human experience. Or, to put it another way, the traditional cultural activity through which communities and societies have supported the moral development of children has been what we now refer to as religion, the universal activity which has always involved beliefs and practices associated with alleged supernatural beings—spirits, gods, God and so on—existing outside of our ordinary, natural experience.

We will investigate the central role of religion in detail in the next chapter, but the contemporary western mind rebels against any notion of supernatural beings, especially the idea of an exclusive one-God who actually exists. Surely, you urge, there must be an evolutionary explanation for the emergence of selfless love? Even if the clear and only really objective evidence at hand is that it never emerges in any individual human's life except through outside intervention, perhaps there is some evolutionary mechanism, lost now in the sands of time, that might hypothetically explain selfless love's general emergence in our species from within rather than from without?

It is a great question in evolutionary theory: the evolution of altruism—the commonly used technical term, as we've noted, for selfless behaviour—in animals. There are very plausible, widely-accepted theories available now for how altruism evolves in non-human animals—in ants and bees, for example, whom we've already mentioned—but we are talking here about non-conscious, instinctive, biologically-based altruistic behaviours. Human altruism, by contrast, might look the same from the outside, but it is actually a completely different thing—conscious, intentional, psychologically-based—and what is going on inside our heads when we (humans) act selflessly makes a world of difference.

We hit a major snag, in fact: Darwin's wonderful theory of evolution, still the cornerstone of our understanding of how life evolves, is based on the pure, automatic, non-conscious self-interest of every individual living organism to survive and survive at all costs, so how can it possibly account for the apparent emergence of the opposite—conscious, intentional *un*self-interest? This is Dawkins' *selfish gene*[4] in action, life reduced to the purely physical, material, a cast-iron mechanical will to survive, incapable, even in principle, of ever breaking out of its own selfish self-interest. Surely, therefore, no matter how we try to explain the emergence of selfless love in evolutionary terms, we are always going to wind up in a contradiction? Thus, initially it might seem there is an obvious individual evolutionary advantage to altruism—the ability to successfully cooperate dramatically improves an individual's prospects and quality of survival—but as soon as you characterise this in terms of personal advantage the contradiction occurs.

Selfless love, in the moment of deciding to act selflessly, involves a letting go of any thought or possibility of personal advantage, even going so far as to be willing to 'lay down your life' for another person—as, for example, a parent might be willing to do for their child, or a patriotic soldier for their country. But such an action could not be subject to any pre-existing biological predisposition or instinct, in fact it would specifically go against any possible biological

---

4. Richard Dawkins, *The Selfish Gene* (UK: Oxford University Press, 1976).

instinct. It would require, rather, a conscious, intentional act of will—for example, the parent would have to see the threat to their child about to occur, then consciously decide to go against their natural instinct to protect themselves from harm, and protect the child instead, knowing that this would threaten their own life.

Any genuine act of selflessness, in fact, from making the 'ultimate sacrifice' to acts which might seem trivial, like holding a door open for another person to pass through first, runs a real, non-zero risk of personal disadvantage which might actually be fulfilled—you might well end up actually dying, or never actually get through that door yourself! So, to repeat myself, no evolutionary theory based solely on personal advantage can possibly, in fact in principle, account for conscious, intentional human altruism.

Of course, you might just want to claim that genuine human selflessness doesn't really exist—that no matter how good, kind and caring a person might seem to be, underlying this appearance of selflessness he or she is really only, self-deceivingly perhaps, and in an interestingly convoluted way, looking after number one. But this flies in the face of experience, of the real, objective evidence of selfless love in operation in the world. Thus, virtually all people are capable of genuine selflessness at least some of the time, and as a result human families, communities and societies mostly work pretty well and even flourish. Eventually democratic forms of social, political and economic life and government emerge which enshrine equality of opportunity and fundamental human rights and freedoms, all of which are based on, at the deepest level, individuals intentionally (if not always unbegrudgingly) limiting their own self-interest in favour of the interest and good of others, and of the community or society as a whole.

We'll look at the amazing link between selfless love and democracy in detail in Chapter 7, but the bottom line at this point is that none of this would have come about—human cooperative life mostly working and often flourishing—if apparent human selflessness was just fakery. So selfless love must indeed be alive and well and out there for real. We're left with the contradiction, therefore—evolutionary theory based on individual self-interest can never account for the emergence of selflessness in human life—and thus the necessity of looking for some sort of outside intervention in order to account for it.

Thank God for that! It is a tantalising thought. Many of us have long since lost, or maybe never had, the ability to find God in our lives or see God at work anywhere in the world—and mostly, about that, we've thought 'who cares', or even 'good riddance'—but at the same time I don't think any of us have ever really wanted to let go of the possibility of genuine selfless love. Now, suddenly, we realize (well, I'm claiming) that the two things—the God who doesn't appear to exist, and the selfless love we hope really does—are inextricably linked. What a quandary!

The fault lies not in our stars, dear reader, but in ourselves: as we will see in subsequent chapters, our amazing success in the evolutionary stakes, our unparalleled ability to not just survive but thrive, is the very thing that blocks us from seeing the God who is the real author of this success—we have knocked God off his pedestal and put ourselves up there instead, and we are all we can now see! No wonder we find ourselves right now in such a fearful state of mind: without intervention from the outside, as we've seen, we can never even escape the closed circle of our own individual selfishness, let alone combat the powerful, destructive cultural forces that seem to surround us in our current polycrisis.

I'm more optimistic, however, as you probably already suspect. But why does it have to be God? The love intervention, as I have argued in this chapter, must certainly come from outside each of us individually—usually from our parents—and, in some real and objective sense, from outside humanity as a whole. So, what exactly is there (apart from a God whose existence we're pretty sceptical about) outside humanity as a whole? If we were to ask this question in relation to any non-human animal, we would probably say nothing except the external, natural environment. But for humans there is something else outside each and all of us, namely the interesting little phenomenon we call *culture*.

Culture: yes, it certainly exists independently of each of us individually, so in that sense it is 'outside' of us, but you wouldn't say that it is outside of us physically, because culture is not really a physical phenomenon, even if it is always expressed and transmitted in physical media. Exactly what sort of phenomenon is culture, then? The word we're looking for is *virtual*: culture is a *virtual* phenomenon. What in the world does that mean? 'Virtual' is a quality we commonly associate, these days, with computer generated VR, *Virtual Reality*, and there is a general sense in the word of some sort of potential or even pretend reality, as opposed to a reality that exists concretely, physically, here right now. Thus, specifically, a cultural artefact like a musical piece, for example, doesn't cease to exist when it is not actually being performed and listened to, rather it exists, in between performances, in a virtual, potential form. The virtual existence of cultural artefacts and culture generally is an entirely objective form of existence, just not physical.

You will have to hold your breath till the next two chapters, where we will explore this notion of culture as virtual in more detail. But how does this work, our interaction with the weird and wonderful virtual world of culture? It goes in a feedback loop: culture starts out inside of us, in our individual human imaginations, our ideas, emotions, dreams, hopes, plans—all, yes, themselves, in the same sense as culture itself, not physical but virtual phenomena, even if they are expressed in the physical medium of the human brain and body. Then these imaginative contents are projected outside of us, expressed in external physical media, shared collectively, acquiring in the process a separate, virtual life of their own, independent of the individual human imaginations they originate in. Finally, culture feeds back into individual imaginations, stimulating more ideas, emotions, dreams, hopes, plans. We are, therefore, both sources and sinks, creators and consumers of culture.

So, outside of us (virtually) there is culture, and it is primarily through this medium that the love intervention we are talking about comes to us. That is our parents for a start—what they've learned from culture in their lifetimes, including especially what they learn from their own parents and bring to the table when they start out parenting. Then, historically, there is religious belief and practice, as we've already discussed, from earliest known times to the present day; the medium *par excellence*, as we'll see in the next chapter, through which the love teaching God we're now surprisingly contemplating the real existence of, intervenes in our lives.

It goes without saying, of course, that if this God, along with all the spirits and gods who came before, is purely a product of human culture—a God 'made in our own image', so to speak—then they do not really exist independently of us, and therefore do not actually qualify as an outside love-teacher. Then, as I have argued, selfless love cannot exist. But it does; so, if God is indeed our love-teaching source, they must exist independently of culture, informing it from the outside—not so much supernatural, in other words, as 'super-cultural'.

Yes, I know, it is all starting to sound rather far-fetched; but, as we have seen, no God, no selfless love; and no selfless love, no possible explanation for the amazing miracle of our survival so far, no hope for our survival into the future. That is why, I am afraid to say, it does have to be God—the very one you successfully vanquished to non-existence long ago, the guiding light of your life, the God who doesn't exist, ever since. But while the love intervention comes to us, collectively, through the medium of culture, then to each of us, individually, through our imaginative experience, culture also contains forces that tend to counteract or oppose its impact, forces we typically refer to by the term 'evil'.

Evil is what human selfishness becomes when we project it outside of ourselves into the collective, cultural sphere, where it acquires a power far greater and more malevolent than mere individual selfishness. Individuals then plug back into this collective power and become capable of things they wouldn't dream of doing as mere individuals—terrible racism, oppression, sexual perversion, criminality, murder, war, mayhem of all sorts—cultural forms of evil which take on such a compelling, virtual life of their own, that they have been taken historically as real beings or agencies, demons, evil spirits, even the devil themself. The virtual space of culture is really where it all happens, the great cosmic battle between good and evil, as imagined by historical religions and contemporary popular culture alike. As we foreshadowed in the introduction, this is what we are really up against in our current polycrisis: not just individual human selfishness, but powerful, destructive cultural forces that feed and amplify this selfishness and now seem to threaten our survival.

I'm sure this won't scare you because you are already scared, you already sense what we are up against. Humans have always had a profound sense of great evil lurking 'out there', ready to possess and destroy us at a moment's notice. Just as we have also always had a sense of the opposite, a great God, a hero, a Saviour who might save us—or maybe it is only hope, wishful thinking, a childish fantasy? But be of good cheer: now for the first time in a long time, or maybe ever, you are seriously contemplating the possibility there really is a hero, a saviour, a God of love out there, one who might prove more than a little useful in helping us out of our present troubles—who even, for all we know, already has the situation in hand. So, hang on to your hats, suspend your disbelief for a little while longer, and turn now to the next chapter and a detailed exploration of the way in which religion works in our lives—where we will start tracking down this enigmatic love-teaching God we have suddenly realised might actually exist.

Chapter 2
The Career of the Gods

We started out this story with a remarkable conjunction: the near complete disappearance of God from the western consciousness just when a perfect storm of trouble is brewing around the globe, a veritable 'polycrisis' of climate change, war, social and political polarization, economic meltdown, pandemic, you name it. God seems to have gone AWOL just when we need them more than ever—because, as we saw in Chapter 1, if there is no real God who exists outside of us, outside of human culture, outside of our own consciousness, we're cut off from the only possible source of the one thing that can save us, namely selflessness, selfless love. Selflessness—some facility with it, some capacity to execute it every now and again—is, I have claimed, the essential ingredient of successful cooperative behaviour in humans; without it, far from lasting long enough to now be facing a polycrisis, we would have almost certainly extinguished ourselves long ago.

Why exactly is God our only hope, particularly one whom, we have recently convinced ourselves, never existed in the first place?! Well, as I argued in Chapter 1, selflessness in humans is a learned rather than natural-born behaviour, and without intervention from the outside by parents in a child's life, and later by other agencies in the surrounding society and culture, to teach it, children will simply never pick it up. The question then was, if selfless love teaching always comes via outside intervention, who or what is there outside of humanity in general to intervene and get selfless love happening in human life in the first place, and keep it happening? The answer was God, acting through the cultural medium of religious belief and practice—or at least that is how humans have understood it throughout most of history, right until very recently. And somehow this seems to have done the trick: selfless love, a real, non-zero amount of it, has come into the world, there's plenty of it around in fact—even if, as I have suggested, we might need an extra big dose of it right now to get us through our current crisis.

We have been practising a little discipline I call 'anti-theology', working backwards from readily observable data to the surprising hypothesis of a God who really exists—I hope you're enjoying the ride! The God we have induced by this process has always been, we now cannot avoid but assume, our only hope. But how exactly has this God, through religion, pulled off the trick of bringing selfless love into the world, of teaching us the art and science of it? A great question: so, let's now take an imaginative journey through the origins and development of religion to see if we can begin to trace the story and solve the riddle. 'Imaginative' is the operative word here, as we saw in the last chapter, for it is through our imagination, our consciousness, that we interact with religious culture, and, beyond this, with the God whom we hope to find *out there*, the one we are hoping to engage as our love-teacher. Religion, both our individual experience and our cultural expression of it, is fundamentally an imaginative or (the word I used at the end of the last chapter) virtual enterprise. Do not look, therefore, for the reality of religion and God in the physical, material world of your direct experience, because you will be sorely disappointed—that is the God who definitely doesn't exist—look instead through the eyes of your imagination; there you might find one who does.

In fact, we have always found the gods in our imaginations. The gods, and God, as we have imagined them, are *supernatural* agencies—and by 'supernatural' here we initially don't mean much more than invisible and immaterial. We cannot see them or touch them, we know them only by the physical effects we ascribe to their agency, by their apparent communications with us through apparitions, dreams, ecstatic visions and the like.

Alongside the gods, religions historically have imagined all sorts of other supernatural agencies—ancestor spirits, spirits of nature, angels, demons, devils, fairies, ghosts and so on—all of which, like the gods, we know only by their effects and their apparent communications with us. Our primary mode of interaction with them is imaginative, even when, as we'll see, we attempt to express or embody them in physical media. But how did we ever start looking for and interacting with such fantastical, slippery creatures in the first place? To answer this question let's now see if we can imagine our way into the minds and experiences of early humans, our own dear ancestors.

> This is the account of the heavens and the earth when they were created, when the Lord God made the earth and the heavens . . . Then the Lord God formed a man from the dust of the ground and breathed into his nostrils the breath of life, and the man became a living being.
>
> Now the Lord God had planted a garden in the east, in Eden; and there he put the man he had formed. The Lord God made all kinds of trees grow out of the ground—trees that were pleasing to the eye and good for food . . . A river watering the garden flowed from Eden . . .
>
> The Lord God took the man and put him in the Garden of Eden to work it and take care of it.[1]

The amazing, familiar, dramatic story of creation from the Hebrew Old Testament. We will come back to it in earnest in Chapter 4, where we will see that the key to understanding it is definitely to not take it literally. Humans were not in fact created in a single once-off act from 'the dust of the ground', rather we evolved from precursor species over at least 300,000 years, as we noted at the start of the last chapter. And the environment we were 'born' into was certainly no garden, rather the same wild, untamed, hostile nature that had confronted all life on earth to that point, with constant competition between and within species for scarce and unreliable resources, survival only of the fittest.

The world of our distant ancestors, therefore, even if there is only very limited information, we can directly glean about it from historical and archaeological evidence, was almost certainly far more difficult, dangerous, unpredictable, uncertain, than the world we experience now. Our ancestors would have had only very limited control over the physical conditions of their existence—the wonderful science, technology and industry we enjoy now, with all the material benefits they afford, were still a long way off, not even yet a pipe dream. Unpredictability was by far the norm: the few things we could control paled into insignificance beside the things we could

---

1. Gen 2:4–15 (NIV).

not, things that could stop us dead in our tracks and kill us in an instant, for example—indeed, what were we to make of the threat of wild animals, extreme weather events, the sudden onset of illness, other human groups whose power might be in a different league to ours?

In the modern world, with science and technology always at our fingertips, we automatically look for physical causes we can potentially control for any physical effects we have not predicted or don't like. If you think about it, however, there are always two ways of explaining why something happens when it happens. Yes, it could be the effect of a physical cause. But it could also be the effect of the intentional action of a third-party agency, either one we can see clearly, like another human or an animal, or one that might be hidden and which we might initially only be able to speculate about.[2]

This is the key point. We have long since stopped ascribing what happens in the world to hidden agencies acting behind the scenes. But do you remember what things were like when you were a child? Mummy and daddy were forever explaining things that happen in the world by personifying them—that is, by depicting them as agencies. All sorts of inanimate and animate objects had smiley or grumpy faces on them. The happy, smiling sun, the man in the moon, the puffy cloud blowing the wind; cars and trains and trucks were living beings not machines, animals and plants had human personalities, even mythical or fictional creatures were embodied and acquired humanness, and the whole world was imagined to be alive with quasi-human agencies operating everywhere. At this point your parents, depending on their cultural and religious background, might also have begun to introduce you to disembodied supernatural or spiritual agencies such as spirits, angels, devils, even gods or God.

As we saw in Chapter 1, we humans are uniquely self-conscious, an experience, we suggested, that is simultaneously an experience of our own self, and other selves, as distinct selves or agents. The impact of this experience on our lives is so compelling that we find ourselves, from an early age, spontaneously looking for and expecting to find agencies everywhere. Thus, little children are very naturally able to

---

2. Richard Dawkins gives the example of hissing in the grass: it could just be the wind, but it could be a lion stalking us. See *The Supernatural Agencies*, <https://www.youtube.com/watch?v=Ho2zDv8lzAM>. Accessed 18 November 2024.

imaginatively identify with the various personifications their parents present to them, and readily enter into the creative subterfuge. Then ensues the endless round of role-playing games that are characteristic of early childhood. Not just parents but anyone or anything else around—pets, dolls, stuffed toys, siblings, friends, extended family—become participants, willing or otherwise, in the child's playful fantasies.

Now, what is the purpose of all this personification and role-playing, which both parents and children seem to engage in quite naturally and spontaneously? Parents initiate it, and, yes, it is certainly deliberate and intentional; but I don't think we have a clear idea in our minds, at least initially, of why we are doing it, except that it seems like a lot of fun and the child typically responds readily and enthusiastically. In fact, however, what the parents are effectively doing is teaching the child how to relate to the world in general, and in particular to the human world—how to cooperate positively and successfully with other agencies or selves in the great game of life.

Specifically, the child, through what might seem on the surface to merely be playfulness, learns, if all goes well, to treat all things, even inanimate objects, with a real degree of circumspection, even care and respect, as if they were all, without exception, real living beings, agencies, essentially human agencies just like themselves. We might go even further and say that the parents are introducing to their child that most essential tool of cooperative living—the very thing every parent is most concerned their child should learn, even if they are not usually particularly conscious of it—namely the capacity, as we have noted a number of times now, for a certain, non-zero modicum of selflessness, of selfless love.

In time, of course, the child also develops his or her skills of practical, physical action—the other thing that always concerns parents—and in so doing learns to distinguish between effects which are the result of physical causes and those that are the result of the action of agencies; and therefore the difference between actual living agencies, like people and animals, and imagined ones. If the child's parents are religious believers, the child might retain into adulthood a belief in some sort of divine, supernatural agency operating in the world; otherwise, by the time it heads out into the world to fend for itself there are no agencies left in its world, natural, artificial or supernatural, other than actual living things.

We are talking about modern children, of course. Back now to the ancestors. The world of human prehistory was obviously very different, as we've noted, to the world children grow up in now, and it's likely that our forebears would have gone through the same phase of ascribing agency to all sorts of phenomena which in reality had physical causes, without the possibility of eventually growing out of it. They would have seen the example of real agencies around them, like other human beings and wild animals, and extrapolated the idea of agency to natural phenomena, including night and day, the seasons, the weather, and so on. Some of these things might have been relatively predictable, but virtually none of them would have held out any prospect of direct physical control. The worst things—floods, earthquakes, droughts, for example—were completely unpredictable. Ascribing some sort of agency—unknown, invisible or at least not immediately evident—to natural phenomena, rather than just seeing them as random events, was a natural and logical first hypothesis, one which opened up the possibility of eventually being able to bring some predictability and degree of control to our dealings with them. Worth a try at least: if these agencies turned out to actually exist there was then surely a chance we could find some way of communicating with them, and thereby to somehow convince them to act more favourably toward us.

We have here now what looks like the worldview of ancient humanity—imaginatively reconstructed to fit my narrative like a glove, you're probably thinking! In the present day, with our scientific mindset, we tend to see only physical cause and effect—which we have largely succeeded in taming—and even actual, living agency, including human agency, is considered, ultimately, to be only an appearance, the non-physical, subjective effect of a physical cause, namely physical processes in the brain. But the worldview of the ancients was teeming with agency, real or imagined, and the choice was an existential one, to either believe in all these agencies—be wary of them and attempt to find ways of dealing with them—or perish!

Right here, in fact, we have the genesis of what we now call religion. The great question our ancestors urgently needed the answer to was, how were they to deal with all these agencies, especially the ones they couldn't see, which we would now say they merely imagined? Well (our ancestors asked themselves), what were these agencies that seemed to rule our lives actually like? They could only be imagined by extrapolation from our own human personas, simply because we have no direct experience of any agency other than our own; so they were, as we imagined them, essentially *like us,* that is, *in our own image.* You can see this in the imagined agencies of modern childhood: Thomas the Tank Engine might have a body that is a machine, but his personality is completely human, with all the normal qualities and foibles of humanness, interacting with a whole lot of other railway machinery likewise imbued with human personhood, as well as with some actual (animated) humans.

Modern parents and other adults use personification, as we have already suggested, to teach children the art of positive interaction and cooperation with others and with the world—including, especially, the amazing little trick of being able to contemplate the possibility that the other is a self just like you, who has more or less the same needs and wants, and whom therefore it would be smart and good to respectfully consider and care about before just barging on in and doing purely what you yourself want. A certain degree of selflessness, in other words, like yeast to make a world of difference. However, in the case of early humanity—that is, humanity as a whole—there was, apparently, no equivalent of modern parents—we were on our own, learning the ropes of life as a species, and the imagined agencies were, moreover, believed to be real, not just pretend.

Or were we—on our own, with no equivalent of modern parents? My hypothesis, as you know, is that we were never actually alone—that there must have been some sort of real God out there all along, whose primary concern was to teach us how to love. But let us imagine for a moment that we were actually on our own, trying to work out what to do about all these agencies we imagined in our own image, who seemed to rule our lives. Without the advantage of the equivalent of wise parents, with all their mature knowledge of what it's like to be a human self, to guide us, the sorts of personalities we projected onto the agencies in question—the gods, spirits, angels, devils and so on of ancient religious traditions—could only have been those of our purely self-centred selves, not yet informed by any degree of real selflessness. And then, presumably, over a long historical period, we must somehow have managed, through our interaction with these completely self-centred and purely imaginary agencies, to teach ourselves how to love selflessly. Go figure!?

But let us keep pursuing the possibility, basically the equivalent of imagining that a human child could pull off the miracle of teaching itself how to love selflessly without any outside help. So, having imagined the supernatural agencies in question into existence—we will explore how we might have managed to do this shortly—with the purely self-centred personalities that we ourselves at the time possessed, the questions we presumably asked ourselves about them were: What do they want? How can we attempt to influence them to operate in our favour? How can we ally ourselves with them in some way?

Remember, these imagined agencies existed alongside all sorts of real agencies, namely, especially, other humans, with whom we were either in constant close contact (our own family and community) and needed to continue developing our skills of cooperative living with, or who belonged to other human groups and presented opportunities, challenges or threats in relation to us, and whom we were concerned also to learn how to best deal with. You might say, therefore, that at this point in our development we were faced with, not just the immediate physical necessity of survival we held in common with all living things, but also with a profound moral or psychological necessity—an urgent, very real pressure to find ways of cooperating successfully with others, natural or supernatural—a pressure, unique to our species, which ultimately boils down to, as we've seen, our developing at least some rudimentary capacity for selflessness.

A tale of two necessities, not one: physical necessity which we share with every living thing without exception, and psychological necessity which is uniquely our own. But the critical question at this point is what exactly do they want, these invisible powers that seem to rule our lives? We can only imagine them as if they are just like us, so we need to ask the question of ourselves: what do *we* want, what do *I* want? I want to, firstly, survive physically, for one more moment, for a long time hopefully. This is the first necessity, physical necessity, and all sorts of evolved biological, instinctive processes—homeostasis, for example, or the fight or flight response—are set up in our bodies and brains to achieve this. But we (humans) are subject also to the psychological necessity I have just described, and this second necessity, over time, becomes all the more urgent, simply because it is *not* subject to any inbuilt evolved, biological processes—as we have already suggested, intentional, selfless, cooperative behaviour is completely unnatural and can only be acquired by learning with outside help.

Now, this second, psychological necessity, the urgent need to find ways of cooperating with others, is a very real evolutionary pressure, in the sense that, as we have noted a number of times, without it *homo sapiens* would have almost certainly extinguished itself long ago. But unless we actually experience this pressure in some way, ourselves, psychologically, we are in trouble. Later in our development what we call a moral conscience emerges (we will certainly come back to this in Chapter 4) which helps us to have second thoughts before we barrel on ahead selfishly and ruin our chances of successful cooperation; but what about before then? How do I now, in the moment, before my sophisticated moral conscience has developed, or cuts in, experience psychological necessity—what does it *feel like*, what does it make me *want*? Well, on one hand, it makes me feel lonely, alone, disconnected from others and the world, like there's something missing in my life; then, on the other hand, it makes me want, yearn to be not alone, not disconnected, to be accepted, liked, loved.

Tell me if this is not how we feel: I experience, very naturally, automatically, a feeling of deficit, of something missing, of disconnection—do other people really like me, or are they really indifferent to me, or even hate me?—is the world itself ultimately against me? This nagging feeling, which I am rarely conscious of, which waxes and wanes in intensity depending on the circumstances of my life at particular times, constantly lures me out of myself in search of connection with others and the world: I am always looking to be liked, loved, to feel the love, to be in a good place with others and the world. We all start out as little narcissists, in other words—it is the natural, default human state—and if you cannot remember what you were like as a little child, just hang around your own little children or grandchildren for a while and you will see what I mean. We would stay this way into adult life, as some people actually do, were it not for the intervention of our parents and others to teach us to not just stare at our beautiful image in the mirror all day long, please!

How does this feeling of deficit, and the automatic response of yearning and looking for love, come about? It is a fundamental consequence of our unique self-consciousness, which we'll explore at length in Chapter 4: in the act of becoming conscious of ourselves as distinct, separate selves, over and against other selves and the world, we experience a severing, a disconnection—me 'in here', everyone and everything else 'out there'—even though, in reality, it is only 'in our minds', that is, imagined or virtual. This places us in an essentially divided virtual state, in which we feel, more or less simultaneously, both the exhilarating power and the terrifying vulnerability of being, or seeming to be, a unique, distinct self. Hence the narcissism: our little severed ego imagines the whole world revolves around it and owes it love and affirmation, at the same time as being terrified that it will somehow never be able to find that love and affirmation.

Now, even though this sounds like a very negative thing—in adult life narcissists are sociopaths who, as we noted earlier, either succeed in life and cause all sorts of damage in their own and other people's lives, or fail and become lonely, isolated figures—the obvious positive side of our natural-born narcissism is that it constantly drives us out of ourselves to connect with others. Then the second necessity we have talked about cuts in again, because in order to connect and cooperate successfully with others long term—in order to get them to give us the love and approval we crave—we have to learn a little selflessness.

It is precisely this natural, narcissistic yearning, then, that we project onto the supernatural agencies that we imagine in the world: just like us they want to be, more than anything in the world, loved. So (we realize, we say to ourselves), if we could just find a way of communicating with them, we might then be able to express our love and deference for them, and that might be a way of getting them to be nicer to us, or at least to not kill us in the next instant. It is the same tactic we would use on a real person who was threatening us—a man with a spear aimed at us, the chieftain of an enemy tribe threatening us with annihilation; we might even try it on a wild beast if worse came to worst. Placate, propitiate, sweet-talk the powers-that-be, in the hope of salvation now or better luck next time—what have we got to lose?!

We can see, therefore, in this way, that when we imaginatively project our own agency onto the unpredictable, unknown phenomena around us, we project with that agency its most definitive characteristic, namely psychological necessity, the deep, burning, unquenchable desire to be, above all else, loved, accepted, approved by others. It is the one chink in the armour, the one vulnerability we can imagine, hope for, of these otherwise completely out-of-our-control powers—that they have the very same Achilles heel, the same fatal fetish, as us.

But there is an immediate, insoluble, deal-breaking problem with this project: we just do not know how to love. We want to get love, to be loved—more than anything, as we have seen—but we have not, at the outset, the slightest idea how to give it. Maybe we could draw on the natural, instinctive love we feel for our parents or siblings; but maybe not because the love we are looking for in this case is, as we described it in the last chapter, a different kind of love, an intentional, selfless love. Thus, we love our parents very naturally and unconsciously early on—it is hard not to, they are everywhere around, physically present to us, catering for all our needs, at this time—but intentionally loving an invisible, supernatural agency that we are never quite sure is actually even there is, obviously, by contrast, completely unnatural!

Remember, at this point in our journey we are still in a 'state of nature', only just emerging as a species, uniquely and suddenly self-conscious; but, in that self-consciousness, at the outset, completely self-focussed, self-absorbed, selfish—and unlike modern children we are without the equivalent of parents who have themselves already learned how to be selfless and who can therefore teach us the art of it. So, what in the world can we possibly do?

This was the burning question, remember—how do we deal effectively with the supernatural agencies who seem to smile on us benevolently one day and rain on our parade the next? But it is not essentially different to the problem we started with (in Chapter 1)—namely, how do we deal with each other, live together cooperatively and fruitfully in families, communities and societies, practice some degree of selflessness in relation to each other? So, agencies: doesn't matter if they're natural like us ourselves, or supernatural, it's the same very unnatural unself-centred love that's required to make some headway with them either way!

In those early days, therefore, long before anything remotely approximating civilisation had emerged, when we still had no idea or experience of selfless love, we could only persist in our efforts to manipulate the unseen powers around us by a show of the love we thought we would want to receive ourselves. Thus developed the many ancient religious systems of obeisance and sacrifice, supplication and entreaty—all focussed on spirits, gods and other supernatural beings who, if they were not actively hostile to us, were still (like us) by nature self-centred, narcissistic, capricious, and definitely in need of being cajoled into acting even remotely in our favour. The best we could hope for was a god of righteous judgement and punishment whose rules and regulations (if we could just work out what they were) we might find it not too onerous to obey; the worst didn't bear thinking about!

Gods made to order in our own image! We were ever in a position of trying to bargain our way into the gods' good books: 'I'll love you if you promise to love me in return.' Where else could we start? Like little children sucking up to their parents to try to get them to give them what they want. When that doesn't work, the real gloves-off manipulation starts!

Religion too always had its *doppelgänger*, in fact, Mr Hyde to its Dr Jekyll, intertwined with it and at first barely distinguishable from it: the weird and wonderful cultural practice of *magic*. In simplest terms, magic is our historic attempt to manipulate the powers-that-be by the opposite of love, that is, by indirect, coercive mind control, by psychological trickery or deceit. We throw anything we can think of at the supernatural beings and forces that seem to rule our lives—spells, incantations, rituals, divinations, magic wands and other devices—in an attempt to force or trick them into doing what we want.

Where in the world would we get the crazy idea that we could manipulate other agencies purely by the psychological force of our own minds? Well, psychological and emotional manipulation is a pretty natural human thing—everything from, yes, flattery and sucking up, to putting people down, making them feel guilty or sneakily undermining them—we cannot help ourselves, we're constantly trying it on each other. So why not try it on the supernatural powers, whom we can only but guess have the same foibles as us? Maybe it is not such a crazy idea.

The fact that we also seem to be able to exercise a degree of psychological control over certain other animal species, in the process of domestication, encourages the strategy further. But the thought of it really originates, I would hazard, at a deeper level, in the amazing experience of self-consciousness itself, an experience that makes us, as the saying goes, 'full of ourselves'. As we have seen, in the moment of self-consciousness we are filled with a sudden over-powering sense of self, and the seemingly unlimited possibilities of our power over the world—even if this is actually no more than a feeling of certainty that we have inalienable control of ourselves—and that, in the final analysis, no one can touch us. 'You cannot tell me what to do, I will do what I want', replies the defiant child to its parent—which turns out, as we all know from bitter experience, to be completely self-defeating.

Initially, however, the magical mind-control approach is not essentially very different from the approach of religion—they are both attempts at manipulation—but in time magic does become distinctive and distinguishable. By the time you get to the era of major world religions, religious authority starts to explicitly repudiate magic as false or evil. The magical approach is always more anarchic, more on the side of immediate, individual gain, the realm of the rebel, the outsider, more interested in manipulating powers of darkness than light, frequently running counter to the goals of authority and society. Religion is, by contrast, as we've seen, always essentially conservative, focussed on cooperation and social cohesion; so sooner or later, inevitably, it must oppose its anarchic alter ego.

The other factor that leads to the gradual repudiation and decline of magic is the obvious one: the rise of science—even if that tends to have the same effect on religion. In the end we give up on magic because, unlike science and technology, it simply doesn't work. Yet despite our modern scientific sophistication we continue to be fascinated by the idea of it—witness the phenomenal success of the *Harry Potter* literary and film franchise in recent years, for example— because the tantalizing possibility of such transcendent individual mind-power remains deeply and primally rooted in our psyche.

Either way, whether we are doing magic or religion, or both— remember, at first, they are not distinguishable—the first thing we need to do, in order to have any prospect of manipulating the supernatural powers-that-be, is find a way of communicating with them. To do this we have to somehow locate and personify them: find bodies, natural or supernatural, for them to put on, and turn them into personas, personalities, real, live beings.

How can we possibly do this, seeing they start out purely hypothetical? Well, obviously a lot of imagination is required. Little children, as we have seen, have no trouble doing it, but the process is entirely dependent on their parents kick-starting it, through play, games, storytelling, picture books and so on. So, who or what kick-starts it in the first place for humanity as a whole?

Our usual question! We might imagine that dreaming—everything from our nightly sleeping dreams, to casual daydreaming, to ecstatic visions or hallucinations stimulated, perhaps, by alcohol or other natural psycho-active substances—played a central role. Dreaming, our subjective experience of it, is a perfect example of what we have described before as virtual rather than physical: we might be (virtually) flying through the Arabian desert on a carpet, while (physically) snoring away to our heart's content in bed. Dreaming generally involves an unconscious free play of our imagination, drawing on our memory for its contents. Memory itself is a pure virtuality, and it includes not just memories of previous conscious physical experiences, but also memories of previous imaginative experiences, either unconscious ones from previous dreaming experiences, or more or less conscious ones from past interactions with physical nature and virtual culture outside of us.

Our dreams: some of my friends claim not to have any, others like me know that we have them but can rarely remember them clearly, usually only the sequences that occur immediately before waking. They seem to be full of mysterious, enigmatic agencies, some of whom we recognise as people we know or have known, but even when they are familiar, they can quickly change into someone or something else completely unfamiliar. We ourselves are always the subject, the central autobiographical character/agency of the dream, and sometimes we seem to be observing these other agencies disinterestedly, but invariably the action centres on us, to the extent that we might seem even to merge identities with another agency. Dreams usually take place in what appears to be a normal physical reality, but this reality doesn't follow normal rules of cause and effect, with the dreamscape constantly changing in nature and location.

Theatrical plays and films, and novels too, while we are reading them and imagining the action of the story unfolding, are obvious conscious counterparts of dreams. What they have in common with dreaming is the constant focus on interaction between characters or agencies in the unfolding story, and even though the characters are other people rather than ourselves, the process of viewing or reading always involves an imaginative identification with one or several of the characters, an identification which may shift from character to character during the course of the story, just as it does in dreams.

Dreams are sometimes recurring, involving the imaginative replay of contents from previous dreams. In my own recurring dream of childhood, a particular one I have remembered all my life, there was an agency in the dark storm clouds that I was terrified of, but I was also angry at it because it would interrupt my play. In the dream I am in the backyard playing, aware of the storm's looming presence and my mother telling me to come inside away from it; but sooner or later I cannot stop myself shouting defiantly at it, 'shut up', the rudest thing I knew to say back then. Then it would glare back at me (I can see its very eyes still) and start to explode with anger, thunder and storm. I would rush to go inside, but my mother was there, standing folded arm in the doorway, very cross at me, and I knew I wouldn't make it. At that point I would wake up in a cold sweat.

No doubt one of my early interactions with the gods of my imagination, my wilful agency and hubris leading inevitably to judgement and disaster! But the agencies we experience in our dreams, appearing and acting in different guises, can surely only be our own agency itself, for what else is there inside our respective heads other than our own individual agency? Thus, our agency, seemingly, is able to re-animate, bring back to life, personas from our memory, even personas from previous dreams and imaginations—like a DVD player re-animating a film, with all its characters, stored in the digital memory of a disc. These re-animated agencies of our dreams may be distinctly recognizable as real people we have known in the past, or they may be transformed by the dreaming process in ways that make them unrecognizable, unfamiliar, perhaps even original.

In the present day we pay little attention to our unconscious dreams, even if we remember them—which we mostly don't—and one reason for this might be that through art and culture we have increasingly found ways of externalizing our imagination, making it a conscious, intentional activity, as producers or consumers or both. There is an outside chance we will find our way to the psychoanalyst's couch at some point in our life for a round of dream interpretation, but mostly we consider dreams to be just dreams: a random jumble and replay of subjective memory, with little or no objective meaning, and at best only an occasional relevance to our conscious life.

In ancient times, however, in a world far more unknown and out of control, far less filled up with the externalised products of human culture, we can guess that dreams were naturally felt to be of real significance. Our ancestors would have had no clear idea where dreams came from, and, in the case of particularly vivid, memorable dreams, might well have seen them as interactions with an objective supernatural world beyond their ordinary conscious experience. Ancient literature is full of recounts of significant dreams and their interpretation—the Hebrew Old Testament alone, for example, has about a dozen dream stories, everyone from Jacob and Joseph to Solomon and Nebuchadnezzar getting in on the act.

So, on one hand we are looking for bodies and personas for the unseen supernatural agencies we think might be operating in the world, and on the other we seem to be 'visited' by all sorts of strange figures, some familiar, some decidedly not, in our dreams. It seems plausible, therefore, that we would have connected the two, so that the enigmatic figures appearing in our dreams would have gone a long way towards providing the virtual embodiment of the invisible agencies. And this is not just a subjective, individual process: we are collective, communal creatures, we dream and imagine together, share the experience, search together for embodiment of supernatural agencies and ways of communicating with them. 'Confabulation'—the modern psychological term for the subjective fabrication of partially or completely false memories without any conscious intention to fabricate—is a nice word we might be tempted to use to describe the process we're trying to reconstruct. But to the ancients the 'discovery' of spirits, gods and so on, would have seemed, to all intents and purposes, a completely objective process.

In terms of dream-appearing figures, the prime initial candidates for supernatural beinghood would surely have been our own close ancestors. Our dead loved ones often appear in our dreams, they are familiar, easy to identify, appearing in multiple people's dreams in the close family and community, and the emotional connection is strong, so that we yearn for them to still be alive and reachable in some way. It is plausible, therefore, to imagine that belief in supernatural ancestor spirits might have been the beginning of traditional religion. Next might have been, for similar reasons, animal spirits, especially those animals whom we have grown to love through domestication, or, conversely, wild, dangerous animals that we fear most intensely— our supernatural world has already by this time acquired a decent-sized population. The next step is nature spirits, which then, as our supernatural world develops a more and more complex and detailed virtual reality of its own, give rise to agencies which exist on a higher, more general, more abstract plane—to what we call gods, in other words. And then there are all sorts of hybrid ancestor-animal-nature-spirits-gods which appear between these main levels.

What keeps driving the development and elaboration of the religious supernatural world in traditional societies? First, new unpredictable things keep occurring, provoking new explanatory agencies that need embodying. Second, attempts to influence the agencies identified and embodied so far, sometimes, or even usually, fail—if only because, as we are assuming at this stage, they do not actually exist. Third, our technology and science develop, so that agencies that were previously believed to exist tend to be replaced by natural causes, thus either becoming redundant (and disappearing altogether) or becoming more general and abstract (more god-like).

The enterprise of locating and personifying these supernatural agencies is always an urgent one, however, because it is only as we can identify them that there is any hope of communicating with them and thereby influencing them to act more favourably towards us. As we gradually abandon our attempt to manipulate the powers-that-be through mind-control (magic), our attempt to manipulate them by love takes over (religion). Our hypothesis, as we've seen, is that they are essentially like us, in that the one thing they want, more than anything, is to be loved. So, we offer them our love: we honour them, adore them, worship them, devote ourselves to them, abase ourselves before them, submit to them, give our lives to them, entreat them, beg them, placate them, make sacrifices to them, propitiate them. You name it, we do anything we can think of doing to let them know how much we love them, to emotionally manipulate them into being nice to us!

We speak to them individually, in our thoughts and prayers; we speak to them communally through rituals of all sorts. At first, we are motivated purely selfishly—it is only their favour we want to receive, and we do not particularly know how to really love anyway. So, as we've seen, we put on a show of love—what else can we do? But we quickly learn—if only because our devotions often or usually don't work—that this is not enough. We have a strong sense that the spirits can pursue us even into our innermost thoughts. Gradually it dawns on us that only truly selfless devoted love will do.

Shock-horror! Only 'truly selfless devoted love will do', but 'we do not particularly know how to really love anyway'. What an understatement! The agencies—the spirits, the gods, God—'pursue us even into our innermost thoughts'—so we cannot hide, even the slightest hint of sin and selfishness will blow our cover, rip off our mask, expose our true, natural, self-centred self. But we just cannot do it, we cannot break out of the closed circle of our self-centredness—this is the essential barrier we keep coming up against—nothing in our history, in our evolution, can show us how to do it. And if the gods, as we are assuming at this point, are purely imaginary, purely constructs of the human mind and culture, not only cannot they help us, our continued belief in them can only bring us to the point of utter futility and despair.

So, yes, we crash headlong, always, again, into an impenetrable barrier, an existential dead-end. The assumption we have been pursuing the consequences of is that the world of the supernatural is simply a figment of our imagination, and that we are essentially on our own here on planet earth, trying to solve the riddle of selfless love, of how we can find ways of living together in the world without tearing each other to bits. The reality is, however, as we have seen, that the thing we are looking most urgently for seems to have actually been found in human history. Somehow many or even most people in contemporary society are capable, at least to some degree, of selfless love—courtesy mainly, we have said repeatedly, of the determined efforts of loving parents. And the fact that any human grouping or society throughout our long history has ever managed to be relatively stable, harmonious and even prosperous is a testimony to the real, objective possibility of selfless love in the world—not (yet) universal and perfect, obviously, but without any of it at all, as we have said, the human species would almost certainly have extinguished itself long ago.

Somehow, therefore, selfless love has found its way into human life, and, most certainly—the conclusion we keep coming to—it can only have come from the outside. So, scary thought to the modern mind that it is, our assumption must be wrong, and we actually aren't on our own—there must be someone or something out there or up there that mediates love into the world, into human life. A 'divine parent', a 'Father God' or an 'Earth-Mother', perhaps? Not just supernatural but super-cultural as well. Invisible, immaterial certainly, and imaginary, yes, but only in the sense that we interact with this unlikely being not physically but through our imaginations.

So, we might write off many or even most imaginative interactions with mysterious agencies as subjective confabulations of memory and culture, but somewhere hidden among them—how can we possibly tell which ones?—there must be some that involve real connection with a God who objectively exists. The history of religions is replete with alleged dreams, visions, revelations from an unseen, supernatural reality, and religious traditions are often founded, as we have noted, on distinctive, original revelations of the divine, but, yes, somewhere amongst this very colourful pile-up there must be some real truth. The question then becomes: how do we discern the fact from the fiction, the objective revelation from the subjective confabulation?

Well, you will have to wait till Chapter 4—where we'll finally start trying to put some flesh on the bones of our eponymous, hypothetical deity, by tracing their story through one particular religious tradition, the Judaeo-Christian—to see if it is a question that can possibly be answered. Right now, however, I sense you are still not convinced that a God with the qualities we have described—invisible, interacting with us primarily through our imagination, focussed on selfless love teaching—can possibly even exist. Probably far from it—I would be surprised if you were.

So far, I have presented what appears to be (if I don't say so myself) a very plausible, logical argument, based on solid evidence, pointing to a God of love who must objectively exist. But, yes, it does seem, to me even, like mere sophistry or sleight of hand. At this stage we still have only a hypothetical God who, just to compound the problem, as we have noted, seems to have gone missing altogether in recent times.

One profound difficulty we have, in our present scientific age, in believing in a God of any sort, is that the universe seems to be entirely, exclusively physical, material, when the God we're looking for is definitely not. We will have to deal with this problem, right now, first, in the next chapter, therefore, before we go any further. You will recall that, at the end of Chapter 1, I introduced you to an objective reality that is, however, completely non-physical, namely the virtual reality of imagination and culture. So, let us now explore this interesting idea of the virtual in more depth: in doing so we will see that a universe which has room in it not just for physical, but also virtual realities, might also have room in it for the God whom we've lately had so much trouble finding.

Chapter 3
A Living Universe

A God not confabulated in our own image, with all our human faults, especially our natural-born self-centredness and plain inability to consider anyone's needs and desires but our own; rather one we could never dream up or invent because we are made, as we'll see in Chapter 4, in their image, not them in ours. An invisible, immaterial God who is wholly *other* to us, utterly outside of us; who interacts us through our imagination; whose primary quality is non-self-centredness, who in fact seems to be the ultimate and only source of it. That is the God we have now realised—well, it has taken us two chapters—absolutely must, objectively exist.

But we have a problem, a big one. As we noted at the end of Chapter 2, the universe we live in seems to be purely, exclusively physical—an apparent fact that is confirmed, as far as we can tell, by science itself. If that is truly the case we are out of luck: no amount of the sort of fancy logical footwork we engaged in in the first two chapters will ever succeed in conjuring up for us an immaterial, imaginary God of love.

What else, you might ask, do we see with our eyes when we look around, other than physical, material objects, living or inanimate, moving, reconfiguring or just sitting still in space? Even what seems to be empty space around us is filled with air, which is just rarefied, gaseous matter. Ultimately, as we learn in high school science, 'all matter is made up of atoms'—atoms, the ultimate little materialists! Later we learn that atoms themselves are made up of even smaller bits of matter—*protons*, *neutrons* and *electrons*—which in turn are, by all accounts, made up of so-called *elementary particles* with exotic names like *quark* and *boson*. Matter, matter everywhere, apparently, just matter and space, purely physical from start to finish.

Fortunately, as we will see in this chapter, this is very definitely not the case: the world we live in is not purely, exclusively physical. In fact, there is a lot more 'out there' than just material objects. The fact that we *see* the world as purely physical—that material objects are, literally, all we see—is telling: evolution has furnished us with a perceptual system, based foremostly on vision, which focusses first on material objects and their movements in space; an essential thing, for obvious reasons, when you are an animal trying to survive, physically, in the world.[1] Then science takes this to the next level by focussing exclusively on the physical properties of things, in order to develop practical ways and means for controlling and manipulating the world, with an endless array of applications which further enhance our survivability—thank you, science!

As we'll see, however, science itself has long since gone beyond the purely physical. Our ordinary perception sits stalled sometime around the seventeenth century, with the mechanical, atomistic world of classical or Newtonian mechanics, while science has moved on now, by the twenty-first century, to the weird and wonderful world of waves, elementary particles, quantum fields and the like, all of which are very definitely not material. We'll find out, in fact, that our world, our reality, far from being monochrome physical, is dual, *physical/virtual*; and that driving its development, its evolution, is a little something we'll denote by the term, *agency*. Inside this humble notion of agency, we will discover the kernel, the possibility, of the lovely God we are looking for.

Sounds amazing! Far from being essentially material, mechanical, dead, the universe in which we live turns out to be a truly *living universe*—hence the title of this chapter. At this point, however, apart from introducing you to what I believe is a richer, more accurate understanding of the nature of the world we live in, we'll only be able to confirm that God is possible—or rather that God is not *im*possible. We'll speculate about God as the ultimate, original agent, the prime mover and sustainer of all things, but it will only be just that: speculation. We will still have only a theoretical, hypothetical God, and you will have to wait till Chapter 4 before we start to put flesh on bone. My aim, at this stage, is simply to remove a profound barrier to our belief in God, namely the crazy idea, always lurking somewhere

---

1. See, for example, Joseph Henrich, *The Weirdest People in the World* (2020; UK: Penguin Books, 2021), 130.

in the backs of our minds, that science has proved God doesn't exist. Crazy, because the reverse turns out to be true: modern science, properly understood, opens up, for the first time, the possibility, perhaps even the necessity, of a God who really does.

A dual world, a world that is physical/virtual; agency the driver of its development; God as the original, ultimate agent; a living universe. Where do we begin? Well, we have used the interesting words 'virtual' and 'agency' quite a few times already in the first two chapters, as you probably noticed, without much fanfare or explanation, as if their respective meanings were self-evident. So, let's begin at the place where we experience these two things directly, at first hand, namely the living organism, you and I. Continuing on our anti-theological schtick from Chapter 1 and 2, we're now, in fact, going to attempt some *anti-science*: rather than just assume, as science typically does, that the physical is all there is, we're going to go back to an earlier point, where we've made no such assumption yet—to the beginning, in fact, to our own existence itself.

Living organisms, what do we notice about them? Well, we are, each one of us, a perfect little microcosm of the duality we're talking about. A single fertilised human egg cell, for example, as it divides and differentiates and grows into you or I, produces both a physical me, my *body*, and a virtual me, my *self*. It's a simple, self-evident duality we experience every moment of every day, and while there is only one obvious word we use for the physical me—*body*—there are, interestingly, many different alternative words we use for the virtual me, for example *ego, mind, soul, psyche, spirit, consciousness, persona, identity*.

My physical body, with all its parts: cells, organs, tissues, bones, blood, nervous system, brain and so on. My virtual self, with all its parts: conscious awareness, thinking, imagination, memory, feeling, personality and so on. Both are a seamless continuity, so the notion of 'parts' is an overstatement; and the two aspects, physical and virtual, are themselves inextricably entwined, enfolded within each other, completely interdependent. The whole thing—the living organism— has a remarkable, seemingly autonomous individuality; it truly is a whole, a self-complete little unity—you and I, and every organism that has ever lived.

Seemingly autonomous individuality: in a word, *agency*. As it is commonly understood, agency, if you happen to have it, is the capacity to do things off your own bat, as if you had a will of your own. Living organisms don't just sit around and get acted on, like rocks and bodies of water, they do things proactively—for example, they grow (in the case of all organisms) and move around (in the case of animals). You wouldn't tell a rock to 'get a life', but human organisms sometimes need to be reminded!

In the last chapter we had supernatural agents, human agents, animal agents. Agency: the capacity to be an agent, to have an individual unity of purpose. In an organism, internal physical and virtual processes—homeostasis, growth, consciousness—and gross motor actions are all coordinated and oriented toward the goal of continued survival, and whatever else the organism has in mind at any point in time. Agency is the driver of the whole show, whether it is cells dividing and differentiating to produce a functioning organ, or you or I are writing an amazing book like the one you're reading now. Organisms are single-minded even when they do not possess anything remotely approximating a mind. It doesn't always work, of course: the moment passes, the body stops working so well, the book doesn't get written, the organism eventually dies. Living agency is a force of nature—it will rule the world one day—but it is a limited, finite force, at least within an individual organism.

A limited, finite force. Agency appears and operates in the world like a physical force, an energy. It has been understood and named in this way from ancient times: as, for example, *chi* (Chinese), *prana* (Sanskrit), *lung* (Tibetan), *ruach* (Hebrew), *pneuma* (Greek), *eros* (Greek), *spiritus* (Latin). In philosophy and science expressions like *conatus* (Spinoza, Hobbes, Leibniz), *will to live* (Schopenhauer), *will to power* (Nietzsche), *élan vital* (*vital impetus*: Bergson), even *autopoiesis* (in biology and systems theory), are used. In English, apart from *agency*, you might say *vitality*, or, in the biblical usages we will see later, *spirit* or *breath*. It is what people might commonly refer to as a 'life force' or 'vital force'. Dylan Thomas writes:

> The force that through the green fuse drives the flower,
> Drives my green age; . . .
> The force that drives the water through the rocks
> Drives my red blood.[2]

---

2. Dylan Thomas, *The Force That Through The Green Fuse Drives the Flower*, 1934, in *18 Poems* (London: Fortune Press, 1937).

But no, Dylan, agency is not actually a force. There is a world of difference. Force is a physical thing, it acts on physical objects, makes them move and change. Living agency certainly employs forces, to its own ends—all the hyper-active internal and external activity of a living organism in surviving, growing, reproducing, moving around and so on—which is why it looks like a force. When a lion suddenly awakens and leaps up at you menacingly, or tree roots grow slowly and rip up big chunks of pavement, there is certainly plenty of physical force happening, but the living agency in the lion or the tree is the cause, the mastermind of the project, not the project itself.

Do you see the difference? Agency is not a physical force, so you cannot detect it or control it directly by physical means—which is why science, as we will see, cannot find it or do anything with it, and simply refuses to acknowledge its existence. Agency is the trigger, but there's no one pulling the trigger, it triggers itself. It is self-causing, a cause in itself—the Latin term is *causa sui*,[3] 'self-cause'. Agency acts both physically and virtually, but it is, strictly, neither. It initiates all the physical and virtual phenomena within an organism—organization, storage and release of energy in cells, mind or consciousness and all the subjective experience that goes along with it—but it exists prior to and acts independently of all these phenomena.

Living agency keeps going outside organisms as well, in the creation of what we know as *culture*. Animals learn behaviours, make tools, develop social structures and modes of communication; humans, fabulously imaginative creatures that we are, as we noted in Chapter 1, then come along and take culture-making to the next level, developing language, complex social structures, religion, art, science, technology, industry and so on. Cultural products have the same dual, physical/virtual structure that living organisms exhibit internally: expressed and transmitted in organized physical media, the meaning, function and operation of cultural products is completely virtual. Just as individual consciousness is embedded within the physical matrix of the brain and body, culture—which you might call 'collective consciousness'—is embedded within external physical structures. Cultural products, indeed, take on quasi-autonomous lives of their own, acquiring a degree of real agency and influence, putting them beyond the direct control of individual human agents.

---

3. The concept used in philosophy, psychology, social science and theology.

I should say living agency '*appears* to exist prior to and act independently of all these phenomena', perhaps? I'm trying to stick just to what we can readily, straightforwardly observe—trying to get you to 'see' life, what it actually is: something that is invisible, but actually right there, in front of our eyes, all the time. Living agency: whence it comes? Who can tell? The egg cell is fertilised, suddenly; the next moment, *as if* driven by an inner agency, a vital *causa sui*, it starts dividing, differentiating; then before too long you have little old you or I. Fast forward, and the collective effort of a whole lot of agents like you and I has created a global culture so complex and sophisticated that it dominates our lives and now dwarfs individual efforts to change or influence it.

Living agency: yes, science, as I have suggested, has a lot of trouble with it—cannot find it, cannot do a thing, directly, with it—because it (science) only deals with physical causes, not things which are already causes in themselves. This is no fault or critique of science, just a recognition of its essential limitation: there will probably never be an end to science's propensity for coming up with physical techniques to enable us to repair, control, influence and enhance living processes, but the one thing science can just never see, never catch in the act, is living agency itself.

Which, however, doesn't stop science from trying to come up with its own explanation for life in terms of purely physical processes. Triggered and supported by favourable environmental conditions, genes, made up of DNA, containing all the 'information' required to build the mature organism, go to work. Organic growth looks to all intents and purposes, as we have suggested, like life doing its own thing; but, no, according to science, it is physical, material processes which initiate and control the whole project, from start to finish. At its deepest level, therefore, life is understood, by science, as a purely physical phenomenon. Where does life come from, then, in the first place, back in the day? Somehow it must, science can only conclude, emerge out of matter.

There is no doubt that evolutionary biology is, and will continue to be, an incredibly fruitful scientific paradigm—in medicine, agriculture, nature conservation and so on—but the notion that life is a purely physical phenomenon is complete over-reach—because there is actually zero evidence for it. In the first place, every single organism we know of emerges out of earlier, parent organisms of one sort or another—everywhere, as in the biblical genealogies, life begets life. Nowhere, anywhere do we observe *abiogenesis*, the spontaneous generation of life from matter—Pasteur famously debunked the idea (in relation to bacteria) in 1859. The idea that life somehow emerged spontaneously in a 'primeval soup' some four billion years ago or so remains purely theoretical, speculative, and only acquires any degree of plausibility when you insist, as science does, that life must be the result of purely physical processes.

Once again, don't get me wrong; science is amazing, wonderful, beautiful, endlessly useful. Its insistence on focussing on purely physical causes is in fact its genius: science is peerless in its ability to develop practical techniques, as we noted at the start of this chapter, for influencing, controlling and manipulating life. It simply cannot, however, account for or explain life's nature and origins.

What about evolutionary theory itself? Does it not give a thoroughgoingly physical account of the evolution of life? Well, yes and no. In Darwin's theory, evolution is the result of random variation and mutation in the offspring of organisms, on one hand, and natural selection of favourable variations and mutations on the other—both, certainly, observable physical processes. Darwinism explains the evolution of life perfectly—surely? But hang on! It definitely does, but only with the addition of a third, critical element—something that is always assumed but rarely explicitly acknowledged.

What is this third critical something? Well, as we noted in Chapter 1, the theory assumes that all organisms, every single last one of them, participate in the 'struggle for existence'—that, in fact, the coordinated internal and external activity of every organism is oriented, first and foremost, towards continued existence, survival. This is Dawkins' selfish gene again, mechanically grinding out its purely self-focussed survival schemes. Without such a default 'meta-instinct' already in place, life would never get past square one—never survive for one more second, let alone get a chance to reproduce and evolve—and Darwin's grand theory would collapse. But what is this third critical element, this meta-instinct for survival at all costs, other than the very living agency we have been talking about?

Whatever you do, it seems, you just cannot get around the hypothesis of *chi, prana, ruach, pneuma, élan vital, spirit, breath, vitality*—not a force, remember, but agency. It's a pretty good hypothesis, to boot, because you can observe it—living agency—in action everywhere, any day of the week, everywhere you look, in all living things, including (I might point out) you and I. It's a pretty exciting hypothesis, in fact; but is it only in the internal and external activity of living organisms, as we've described, that we see physical/virtual duality? Is everything else just plain physical? Does agency, the producer of this dualism, only operate on a relatively small scale in our universe, confined perhaps to organic life on the surface of planet Earth? In fact, as we'll see now, no, no and no: we can observe the same pattern operating everywhere we look in the universe. It is, in this sense, as we are about to now see, a truly living universe.

What we've noticed about living agency (or *chi, prana, ruach, élan vital*, etc) is that it animates physical matter, brings it to life, organizes it, makes it do things. From a purely physical point of view, it does this by organizing matter into structures (biomolecules, cells, organs, bodies) which are able to store physical energy then release it in a controlled, coordinated way. This is truly the 'miracle of life'.

The controlled storage and release of energy: we see these two modes or directions of energy flow, which living organisms exhibit, everywhere in the non-living world as well. The terms we're looking for are *potential* energy and *kinetic* energy. Potential energy is energy stored, and the fundamental way that energy is stored is by organizing matter. Kinetic energy is energy actually happening, being expended; the simplest example is the energy acquired by a material object when it is set in motion. Typically, we learn about the two forms of energy in high school science.

Potential energy is *virtual* energy, energy that is not in action now but might be later. Thus, for example, organisms store (for later) energy in the form of certain biochemicals (glycogen, triglycerides) in their cells, then they either expend the energy, by converting it to kinetic energy, for their own use—internal activity or motor actions—or bequeath their bodies for energy expenditure by other organisms later, for example food to eat, wood to burn, or, later still, fossil fuels to burn.

In the non-living world analogous processes abound. Chemical potential energy is stored in the organized structure of chemical bonds in all substances, so that, for example, when you judiciously add some heat to gunpowder a whole lot of potential energy gets very quickly converted to kinetic energy in the form of an explosion. Or energy is stored in the organized internal structure of atomic nuclei, with the later release of tremendous amounts of kinetic energy in reactors, bombs or stars. We can store energy by stretching a spring, or in batteries by setting up an organized structure of chemical ions, or by intentionally storing in reservoirs water which would normally flow away into the environment.

And so on. Staggering amounts of virtual potential energy are stored in the organized structure and motion of celestial objects, for example the planets in our solar system orbiting the sun—you can imagine the kinetic calamity that would occur if the earth slowed down in its orbit and started spiralling towards the sun! Then, in turn, galaxies have organized, internal structures, with typical features like an overall disk shape, spiral arms, a halo, a nucleus and a corona, storing even more mind-boggling amounts of energy. Perhaps even the universe as a whole has an organized internal structure, although we may not be quite up to imagining that yet!

Speaking of the universe, we are used to picturing it in our minds not as something that has structure, rather as a whole lot of tiny pinpricks of matter (even the biggest stars) randomly arrayed in a vast expanse of empty space. Not only does the universe not seem to be organized, it seems to be mostly nothing; across those vast expanses of empty space, how could there be anything organizing it and holding it together? But there actually is, according to science, something holding it all together and giving it structure, that is continuously present everywhere, filling up all that emptiness so that it is actually far from empty—something invisible that we just cannot see: the *gravitational field*.

The force of gravity, gravitational force, the gravitational field: we all experience it, happy that it keeps us from flying off a spinning earth, but not so happy when we fall and break a limb. Not just gravitation: from a scientific point of view, it is fields all the way up and down in the universe. Gravity holds things together on the grand cosmic scale; electric and magnetic fields hold bulk materials, crystal structures, molecules and atoms together; quantum fields hold atomic nuclei together. Fields are the invisible glue that everywhere, at all levels, make things stick together in organized structures rather than just drift apart. Maybe there is a single underlying field in the universe, the mother of all fields—Albert Einstein and Stephen Hawking are famous names who spent time searching for it—but despite some promising starts, the so-called *Unified Field* or *Theory of Everything*[4] has remained elusive to this day.

---

4. Variously known as *Unified Field Theory*, the *Theory of Everything* (associated most closely with Stephen Hawking) or *Grand Unified Theory*.

If you want a nice fictional example of a field, try *The Force* in the *Star Wars* film franchise: part scientific, part religious, with a 'dark side' and a 'light side'; a moral, mystical angle as well as a physical. But what exactly is a field, gravitational or otherwise? Well, we know fields only by their effects: if you place a material object in a gravitational field, for example, it will experience a force which makes it do something like drop to the ground, in so doing acquiring a certain amount of kinetic energy. Fields, generally, are pure virtual objects, continuous three dimensional 'wells' or sources of potential energy—like *The Force* in Star Wars, fields are there, everywhere, all the time, we just have to know the right actions or magic words to unlock and activate their potential.

In so-called quantum field theory (now we are at university level physics) all is field, all is virtual. There is, strictly, no longer any such thing as a material particle, as matter: electrons, bosons, quarks and other elementary particles are now *quanta*, localised little bundles of pure waveform, pure energy—like whirlpools in a stream, looking for all the world like discrete objects, but actually relatively stable, dynamic structures or patterns in the whole flow of the water. Our normal way of perceiving and thinking the world reduces everything to material objects moving and reconfiguring in space—what is commonly referred to as a *mechanistic* world-view—but this is a reverse reductionism: everything is reduced to action, continuous flow, energy, and underlying it all is the pure virtuality of the field. May the *Field* be with you, sisters and brothers!

You're getting the picture, I hope. A *Theory of Everything* might turn out to be a bridge too far—the scientific idea of a field is a human 'mental map', a very useful theoretical tool in certain limited practical contexts—for calculating the orbits of planets, for example, or for analysing and controlling electromagnetic or nuclear phenomena—but, as the saying goes, *the map is not the territory*—reality will always be more than any possible map we can ever make of it. Nevertheless, the overall picture is compelling: at all levels of our universe, from the ultra-microscopic to the inter-galactic, with organic life somewhere in the middle, we see the same duality—the same continuous dynamic interplay between the physical and the virtual, between material objects and fields, between potential and kinetic energy.

The same duality, the same dynamic interplay. What initiates, triggers, drives this interplay, however? In the case of organic life, we have already identified a likely culprit: living agency. This sort of agency operates, as we have said, in a limited, localised form in individual organisms during their short lifetimes; but somehow it is also a lot more than this. A little matter of reproduction, then evolution: somehow, through these processes, living agency seems to be able to cheat death, multiply and fill the earth, becoming more and more sophisticated, more adept at surviving and taking control of its own life, as it goes along. Reproduction and evolution operate virtually as well as physically—through the development of consciousness and culture-making as well as biological body-building—so that, from a zero-point estimated at some 4.5 billion years ago living things now cover, dominate and, as we've seen, even threaten the entire planet. So, while living agency might be, from an individual point of view, limited in its impetus, from a collective point of view it seems to be effectively unlimited.

'This sort of agency': living agency operates to produce living organisms, but some form of agency must be at work at all levels in our universe, bringing about the formation of the organized physical/virtual structures we've talked about—everything from nuclei and atoms to planetary and solar systems and galaxies—as well as, from a quantum field point of view, triggering the creation and annihilation of particles or quanta within continuous fields. *General agency*, I'm tempted to call it—of which living agency is a special, distinctive case, perhaps?

'Some form of agency *appears* to be at work at all levels . . .', I should say. Again, I am just trying to work from what can be easily and readily observed, any day of the week. Whatever it is—this general agency in a variety of particularized forms—it certainly cannot be, as we have noted, reducible to any purely physical, material process, because it is what creates physical matter in the first place. If you don't believe me—that matter is created, *ex nihilo* so to speak, out of something that is not matter—and you're not convinced by easily observable phenomena like a tiny seed growing into a giant tree or a single animal cell growing into great big elephant, then believe science. Believe science's very own creation story, in fact, the *Big Bang*.

Yes, *the* big bang, although not really a loud explosion, as we'll see shortly. This is how the story, informed by insights on the interesting little phenomenon of agency we have just garnered, goes. In the beginning, a lazy 13.7 billion years ago, the cosmos is at zero-point, the *Big Bang singularity*—space doesn't exist yet, let alone matter; time itself has not started. The singularity is conceived of as a state of very high density and temperature—in theory, infinite density and temperature. This is pure virtuality: amazing, red-hot potential for something to happen but nothing (yet) actually happening. Then suddenly something does, but it is not an explosion of matter (which doesn't yet exist), as we commonly imagine it, and as the name implies; rather the universe simply starts expanding, completely silently, from the zero-point. As it expands it cools, and in time material particles and then atoms start to emerge, and, later, eventually, planets, stars and other celestial bodies.

Material particles emerge? How so? Well, it is not so much that pure, empty space on its own starts expanding at the Big Bang, rather it's the *field* with the space, or perhaps *as* the space; the two are not in any way distinct. 'The field'? In the latest theories, the four currently described fields—electromagnetic, strong nuclear, weak nuclear and gravitational—are assumed to be unified as one in the initial phase of expansion. And it is out of this unified field that material particles, tight little bundles or whirlpools of energy, start to emerge—as we described above.

May the field be with you—still! But what triggers this emergence of matter out of the unified field? For that matter, what triggers the Big Bang in the first place, the expansion of space from the zero-point singularity? From a scientific point of view the trigger, either way, can only be a physical process, and, in the case of the initial expansion, is presumed to be a completely random 'quantum fluctuation', a highly improbable event that eventually, sooner or later, somehow, just has to happen. Generally speaking, random quantum fluctuations are seen as the trigger for all particle emergence.

Unknown, in other words: we cannot possibly say, from a purely scientific viewpoint, what caused the Big Bang, and what causes the emergence of matter generally, these are just random events that happen to happen. Well, all the evidence we have points, as it turns out, to the precise contrary: not random fluctuations at all, but very un-random agency. All the evidence: we certainly don't see what actually triggered the Big Bang (no smoking gun in sight), and we also don't see what triggers the emergence of organised material structures such as nuclei and atoms, let alone solar systems and galaxies. But we do see, all the time, all over the place, what triggers the emergence of organized material structures in living organisms. Agency—living agency—*chi, prana, ruach, spirit, breath* and so on and so forth. Not only do we see this agency in action, we *are* this agency, you and I, each one of us, inside ourselves, *as* ourselves.

Now we are really over-reaching, leaning into and right over the edge perhaps! What possible agency could have triggered the Big Bang? I think you can see where I am going. Yes, perhaps it was a random fluctuation, but that's really a non-answer, a lame default forced upon you by your insistence, despite all the obvious contrary evidence I have lain before you, that physical processes are all that exist. The only serious, real, plausible answer, however, is the one I have already given: outside intervention by an external, supernatural agency, the God who (you say) doesn't exist.

Let us now, for a moment, for purposes of comparison, go to a different, much older source of information on how the world started out: the well-known biblical narrative on the subject of creation, this time right to the start of the story. We have:

> In the beginning God created the heavens and the earth. Now the earth was formless and empty, darkness was over the surface of the deep, and the Spirit of God was hovering over the waters. And God said, let there be . . .[5]

'Now the earth was formless and empty . . .' sounds pretty much like the pure pregnant virtuality in the split-instant before the Big Bang, imagined by a people, more than three thousand years ago, not yet cognizant of general relativity and quantum field theory. '. . . and the Spirit of God was hovering . . .': we might even take that more or less literally—some significant act of cosmic agency about to make it all happen, apparently. The biblical writers were expressing the distilled wisdom and insights of countless generations before them, all the way back to the unknown and indeterminate dawn of *homo sapiens*—maybe science is now catching up to them!

---

5. Gen 1:1–3 (NIV).

The apostle John a thousand years later was informed also by Greek philosophy:

> In the beginning was the Word, and the Word was with God, and the Word was God. He was with God in the beginning. Through him all things were made; without him nothing was made that has been made.[6]

A little bit further on John makes the critical connection: 'The Word became flesh and made his dwelling among us.'[7] 'The Word' is none other Jesus Christ: initially, at the creation, the divine 'word' of God[8] through whom God 'speaks' all things into existence; eventually, by the time of John, becoming human flesh in the person of Jesus of Nazareth.

The Word: in Greek, Λόγος, the *Logos*. In classical philosophy the word sometimes referred simply to rational discourse, reasoning, rhetoric,[9] but at other times took on a grander meaning as a sort of generative link between divine being and the rational ordering of the cosmos.[10] The latter is clearly the sense in which the apostle is using the word.

The Word, the Spirit: well, yes, agency, divine agency—described by the biblical writers as initiating the creation of the cosmos, or, to put it in modern scientific terms, triggering the Big Bang. Plausible, you'd have to say: if such an agency exists, surely initiating a big bang is just the sort of thing they would do?!

This is only the beginning, however. Very quickly, as we have seen, tracking forward in time from the initial triggering event, material particles start to emerge out of the pure virtuality of the still unified field. Right from the outset, these are organised structures: nuclei and atoms, condensing gradually into stars and planets and other heavenly bodies with their own internal organization, forming into planetary and solar systems, then clusters and galaxies and so on. You don't get matter, at any level, without organised structure.

---

6. Jn 1:1–3 (NIV). Also, Heb 1:3: 'The Son is the radiance of God's glory and the exact representation of his being, sustaining all things by his powerful word.'
7. Jn 1:14 (NIV).
8. The second person of the Trinity, the 'Son of God'; sometimes referred to as the 'Universal Christ' or 'Cosmic Christ'.
9. Plato and Aristotle, for example.
10. Heraclitus, then later the Stoics, for example.

All this emergence and organisation? How so? It can only be the result of some form of agency at work. Original divine agency continuing to intervene in a continuous, systematic way; or perhaps the current of agency injected into the singularity at the beginning is so profound that it continues under its own steam to gradually fabricate the cosmos as we know it? Who could say? Yes, this is certainly over-reach, wild speculation. But what is the alternative? Purely random quantum fluctuations accidentally delivering all that organization? You are the one who is dreaming!

Eventually, we get organic life, at least on one particular small planet we know of. This is definitely something new. Organisms, as we have seen, and as you can observe any time you want, exhibit an individual agency of their own. Every single organism is a little supernatural agent, a little god of its own, doing its own thing, being its own master, although hemmed in on all sides by a hostile physical environment, and with a singular lack of ambition, at least at the outset, to do anything but survive for one more instant. A little god of its own: somehow, in organic life, the agency that we might have described as purely divine, invisible, acting 'from the outside', becomes explicit, separated out, multiple, localized, embodied in individual organisms; while, somehow, as we have seen, at the same time, retaining, through the processes of reproduction and evolution, both physical and cultural, a very real collective form of the original unity it started out as.

This is a remarkable development: again, is it the result of a new, special intervention by the divine agent—'Stop Press, 4.5 billion years ago: God creates life today!'—or is it a continuation, an inevitable outcome of an original, primordial current of agency from the beginning? Again: who could possibly say? But then, continuing on with the story, the next remarkable thing occurs with the emergence of *homo sapiens*: the unique capacity for self-consciousness. We have already contemplated this at length, and there will be plenty more to say about it in succeeding chapters. Humans become *as* gods—at least that is the contention of the serpent in Genesis 3:5,[11] as we will see in the next chapter—and develop the capacity to act consciously,

---

11. 'For God knows that when you eat of it [the fruit of the tree that is in the middle of the garden] your eyes will be opened and you will be like God, knowing good and evil.' (NIV)

intentionally, raising their eyes to ambitions higher than mere survival—like working out how to dominate all other species and the planet, or perhaps just how to get other people to be nice to them sometimes (the subject of this book, no less).

Yes, we'll have a lot more to say about all this—God the original divine agent who started the ball rolling in the first place, the emergence of matter, then life, then self-consciousness and humans as little gods trying to work out how to live together—very shortly. In this chapter, however, my aim has simply been to present a plausible, even compelling argument for the real existence of a little thing called agency, a certain apparent wilfulness or intentionality at play in the universe. Agency—*general* agency, I have dared to refer to it as—which appears to drive the development or evolution of things, existing independently of and creating the physical/virtual duality of our universe.

Physical/virtual duality: you will remember we started out this chapter in a universe we thought was purely, exclusively physical, but very quickly, following the model of living organisms, we realised that, no, our world, far from being mono-culture physical, is a living dynamic duality. But it takes two to tango, and, yes, I have used the word 'virtual' in this context freely, repeatedly, as if its meaning and what it refers to were self-evident.

You are assuming that the other partner in this duality, the 'physical' or 'material', is already self-evident, of course, which may or may not be the case—I would challenge you to come up with a definition of it at a moment's notice! But 'virtual'? I have used the word in three specific contexts. First, the virtuality of a living organism is (in the case of human beings) the subjective self with all its contents—conscious awareness, thinking, imagination, memory, feeling, personality and so on—as opposed to the physical body (or, rather, in concert with the physical body). Second, the virtuality of culture, created by organisms, especially by humans, is the meaning and function of cultural objects, as opposed to the forms of physical media in which they are expressed and communicated. Then third, in modern physics, the virtuality of the non-living universe is embodied, on one hand, in organized material structures like atoms and galaxies; and, on the other, in the form of continuous fields, pure immaterial wells of potential or virtual energy—like the fictional *Force* in Star Wars.

My use of the word (virtual) in these contexts might be unfamiliar or even surprising to you, but I hope you are starting to make connections. What will be very familiar to you, however, as we noted at the end of Chapter 1, is virtual as in VR, *Virtual Reality*. In this context, virtual is usually understood to mean pretend, simulated, fictional, imaginary, fake, artificial, subjective. The connection to cultural objects and subjective experience may then be evident to you: VR might be computer generated, but the experience itself, the virtual aspect of it, is essentially the same sort of thing. The expression 'virtual *reality*' is telling: the experience is absolutely real, but not physical reality, rather an essentially different kind of reality to that of the physical.

Yes, it (the experience) certainly is pretend, simulated, fictional, imaginary, fake, artificial, subjective, but it is completely real: you really are having an experience of mountain climbing in the Himalayas even though you are actually in your lounge room with a pair of VR goggles on—it is an *as-if* experience, but its *as-if*ness is absolutely real. You really are thinking those thoughts, imagining a conversation with your boss over a pay rise; the dream you had last night, even though now you have only a vague sense of its contents, was a real experience; you really do feel elated or terrible right now, as you read this book, you are not just imagining it; that painting, or film, or novel, or football game, has an absolutely real meaning and function in your life and mine, over and above the physical medium it is expressed in.

And then there is what is now probably the greatest cultural virtuality of them all, the World Wide Web, the now ubiquitous virtual reality we spend so much of our time interacting with. Yes, our interaction with the Web is entirely dependent on computers, complex physical machines, but what we do on the internet, the content, meaning and purpose of it, is entirely, objectively virtual.

I doubt I can go any further, dear reader, in explicating the meaning of 'virtual' to you, because, simply, that is exactly what you and I actually do: we are living agents continuously creating physical/virtual lives within ourselves, in continuous interaction with the duality of physical/virtual, nature/culture, outside ourselves. Relative to physical reality the virtual always starts out as a potential, as-if, would-be, could-be reality, which might then, through the action of agency, be actualized and become physical. And relative to virtual reality the physical always starts out as an actual, concrete, already existing present reality which might then, through the action of agency, be ordered, organized and transformed, locking away virtual meaning and potential functionality.

You can think of the physical and the virtual as intersecting, co-dependent realities which are, so to speak, 'enfolded' within each other.[12] But however you think of it, there is nothing obscurely philosophical, technical or esoteric in the duality we're talking about—it is just the day-to-day, prosaic, mostly pretty hum-drum reality of our lives in the world—it has been there all along, in fact, as I hope you have now realised.

But be careful, be warned: once you acknowledge and start to become more aware of physical/virtual duality, and the role of agency in producing and driving its unfolding evolution, you're in grave danger, on a slippery slope, you are beginning to open yourself up, shock-horror, to the possibility of God, the ultimate agent! You might not want to go there—or maybe you do? We are at that point, at any rate. I have proved to you (if I don't say so myself) that God must, logically, hypothetically exist—it is the only explanation for the presence and persistence of real, objective, selfless love in the world—and I have now shown you that our universe is not dead, mechanical, purely physical but alive as live can be. So, it is now time to start trying to put some flesh on the bones of our hypothetical love-teaching deity.

Yes, a real God, to teach us how to love. Why do we need such a God, such a teacher? Because the selfless love we are talking about is not natural, we are not born with any innate natural capacity for it, we have to learn it, someone has to teach us. As we saw in Chapter 1, we have to go against our nature in order to practise it. What is our nature? Self-centred, self-focussed, self-absorbed—that is our nature, our natural self. This is not such a bad thing in itself, however, and it has served non-human animal life well. But when life gets to us, *homo sapiens*, the amazing capacity for self-consciousness cuts in, and at this point, as we foreshadowed in Chapter 1 and 2, and as we'll see now in detail in Chapter 4, all our problems begin. Suddenly a creature that can sin has arrived on the scene. Sin?! Help!

---

12. See, for example, David Bohm, *Wholeness and the Implicate Order* (London: Routledge and Kegan Paul, 1980).

Chapter 4
What's so Original about Sin?

Enough anti-science—hope you enjoyed the ride—let us get back to some good old anti-theology. Our aim, in this chapter and the subsequent two, is to, as we've expressed it, put some flesh on the bones of our hypothetical, invisible love-teaching deity, the one we demonstrated the possible, likely or even necessary existence of in the first three chapters of this book. The anti-theological approach we are taking is simply, you will recall, an attempt to work backwards from plain facts of existence to the elusive God in question who is, we are hoping, the author of them.

In this chapter I am going to reference the creation stories at the beginning of the Hebrew Old Testament, in the book of Genesis, in detail. One thing we must be crystal clear on from the outset is that there is no literal Garden of Eden, no original Original Sin, no Fall with a capital F, no Adam and Eve, no serpent, no fig leaves. Why? Because we believe in evolution, that humans weren't created in a once-off event, rather they emerged gradually out of an evolutionary background of precursor species. If we make the mistake of taking it all literally, we'll find ourselves going down one of two rabbit-holes: fundamentalist creationism, which gets bogged down in this first part of the biblical story and in doing so sets itself up to radically misinterpret the great climax the story eventually gets to; or another sort of fundamentalism, scientific atheism, which spurns the Garden story altogether, rejecting it as a meaningless fantasy concocted by primitive people who knew no better. Either way, we will fail to learn the amazing, critical life-lesson it teaches us.

So, please, let us not take it literally, the Garden story, and see what we have to learn from our ancestors. What we read in the ancient stories—accounts in the Bible, and similar narratives from other traditional cultures around the world—is a distillation of wisdom and insights passed down from generations beyond memory, countless thousands of years before the development of written language. We can only assume that the writers of the stories believed them to be, at the time of going to press, literally true. But even though we know now that cannot be the case, what is important in the stories, anyway, is their attempted explanation of key aspects of the human condition, which, we might hope, is independent of the question of their historicity.

The Garden story, which we are about to turn to, is an early attempt to address the most pressing of all questions: what in the world is wrong with us? Why are we, on one hand, amazingly creative, intelligent, powerful, dominant over all other creatures, undisputed rulers of the earth; but, on the other hand, selfish, destructive, always or far too often in conflict within ourselves and with each other. Why we continually suffer at the hands of our own sinful self-centredness, in other words, why we so often fall victim to our own folly.

What's so original about sin, then? Nothing, obviously! It has always been our Achilles' heel. Sin is nothing more than natural human selfishness, the very thing, we have repeatedly seen, that gets in the way of our ability to cooperate with each other. In composing the story of Adam and Eve the biblical writers were, therefore, responding to the very real evolutionary pressure the problem of sin exerts on us—it is overcome our predisposition to sin and learn to cooperate selflessly together, or perish!

What sin is not, however—and this is a critical misapprehension we will keep returning to—is a problem, merely, of disobedience, of failing to obey a set of rules, even if we're convinced they have come from God themselves.[1] Mere disobedience: the problem we face is, unfortunately, much trickier than that—just ask any parent confronting the daily task of teaching their darling child a little bit of care and consideration of others! If sin was just a matter of disobedience, we will see, there would have been no need for the God whose plan for saving us we are now going to track, to eventually take the amazing, radical step we will read about in Chapter 6.

---

1. The common dictionary definition of sin, for example: 'an immoral act considered to be a transgression against divine law' (Google: Oxford Languages).

Sinful selfishness—but it gets worse! Our individual selfish sin goes out into the collective, cultural space around us to form the various forms of evil that influence our lives, that feedback malevolently and amplify our individual selfishness, when we open ourselves up to them. Racism, oppression, sexual perversion, criminality, violence, murder, war—you will remember the list from Chapter 1, to which many more pathological cultural forms could be added, many of which, as we also noted back then, have been taken historically as real beings or agencies, the demons, evil spirits, even the devil themself, of traditional religion and folklore. So, the problem of sin is also, equally, at precisely the same time, the problem of evil.

Let's now dive into the biblical narrative in earnest, starting a few days on from where, as we saw in Chapter 3, 'God created the heavens and the earth'. The critical moment we're most interested in occurs on Day 6, the creation of humans:

> [26]Then God said, 'Let us make humankind in our image, in our likeness, so that they may rule over the fish in the sea and the birds in the sky, over the livestock and all the wild animals, and over all the creatures that move along the ground.'
>
> [27] So God created humankind in his own image, in the image of God he created them; male and female he created them.
>
> [28] God blessed them and said to them, 'Be fruitful and increase in number; fill the earth and subdue it. Rule over the fish in the sea and the birds in the sky and over every living creature that moves on the ground.'[2]

'In our image': this is the famous *imago dei*, the image of God. At this point in the story there is no explanation of exactly what the *imago* is: the only clue given, in verse 28, is that it is somehow associated with humanity's rule over all other creatures and over the earth. Biblical scholars argue over the meaning of the *imago*, in literary, cultural and historical terms—is it human reason, personality, free will, intelligence, the capacity to relate directly to God; is it something that makes us God's representatives on earth, his 'vice-regents'?.[3] But

---

2. Gen 1:26–28 (NIV).
3. See, for example, GJ Wenham, *World Biblical Commentary, Volume 1, Genesis 1–15* (Texas: Word Books, 1987), 29–32.

the next part of the story—the account of the Garden and Original Sin—provides the context which clearly explicates the meaning of the *imago*. It is amazingly obvious, in fact.

What in fact is unique about human beings, over and against all other creatures? We (*homo sapiens*) are animals, obviously: bipeds, class *mammalia*, order *primates*—nothing especially unique in that. Physically, biologically we are much the same as our close evolutionary relatives. But it is what we *do* that makes us stick out like a sore thumb: we create language, culture, civilization; science, art, technology, industry. We are the only creatures who develop a belief in God then decide God doesn't exist! And, yes, we rule and dominate the earth and all other creatures absolutely, just like the biblical story says.

The usual explanation for this staggeringly obvious uniqueness is that we human beings are just a bit more intelligent than our closest rivals. As if just a little bit more of something, or anything, could make all that difference—as if, in other words, a difference in degree could lead to what is surely a difference in kind? The thing that truly makes us one of a kind is, in fact, as we have already suggested, our uncanny ability, through no fault or effort of our own, to be self-conscious, to be aware of ourselves as separate and (seemingly) self-complete selves.

CG Jung, the great psychoanalyst, in a 1959 television interview, describes the experience beautifully: reflecting on his earliest memory of self-conscious experience, which occurred while walking to school one misty morning at age eleven, he explains:

> I stepped out of a mist, and knew 'I am', 'I am what I am'. And then I thought, 'what have I been before?' And then I found that I had been in a mist, not knowing to differentiate myself from things, I was just one among many things . . .. As far as I can remember, nothing had happened before, that would explain this sudden coming to consciousness.[4]

The first mist is literal, the second metaphorical, as I am sure you have realised.

---

4. CG Jung, interview on *Face to Face*, 1959, at <https://www.youtube.com/watch?v=2AMu-G51yTY&t=46s>. Accessed 18 November 2024.

Jung went on in the same interview to describe how this first conscious experience of his own self-hood seemed to coincide with his first conscious experience of others as selves: he began to notice, for the first time, the fallibility of his parents—they too were selves, like him, with the same sorts of weaknesses and faults. Such early formative experiences were perhaps instrumental in setting Jung off on his remarkable life-long quest to understand what it means to be human.[5]

Unique human self-consciousness: apart from reflecting, like Jung, on your own experience, you can observe it any day of the week by, for example, watching a young human child interact with a pet cat or dog. It's clear that, even at a very young age, and with a far lesser command of motor skills, the little *homo sapiens* is on a different plane of consciousness—the sparkle of self-awareness appears in the eyes and facial expressions of the child in a way that it will never appear in those of their beloved pet. The uniquely human smile—tell me when was the last time you caught a cat or a dog or a crocodile smiling—is perhaps the first moment, the clearest sign, of real self-consciousness.

Self-awareness provides us with the ability to reflect on ourselves as selves, on our own thoughts, feelings and experiences: it is the beginning of the whole human story, our amazing culture-making ability—language, religion, art, science, technology, society and so on—and our dominance, for better or worse, of the planet and all other living species. This is surely what the writers of Genesis were getting at with their revelation of the *imago dei*. They had a profound sense that there was something special about us, something that made us *like* God, that seemed to give us special power to lord it over the rest of creation, even if they couldn't put their finger on exactly what it was—although, as I have already suggested, and as we'll see shortly, the next part of the story takes us closer to the truth, a little matter of 'knowledge of good and evil', then feeling self-conscious about being naked! There is nothing more galvanizingly self-consciousness inducing than, we will soon realise, that pesky conscience of ours.

I am sure I have not convinced you yet about our unique self-consciousness, however; it just sounds too simple to be true.

---

5. See, for example, the collection of essays, *Modern Man in Search of a Soul* (London: Kegan Paul, 1933).

Remember we are telling an evolutionary story, trying to find an evolutionary interpretation of the biblical story, which we know carries amazing wisdom without being—or precisely because it is not—literally true. There is no doubt that human self-consciousness is, on one hand, a continuous development from, an expansion of, the consciousness of higher animals. We are, you might say, just better at it (consciousness). But no, on the other hand, self-consciousness is on a whole other level, a quantum leap beyond animal consciousness, a difference in kind, not degree, in quality rather than quantity.

How could life have made such a leap across a gap? In the biblical account it is the result of specifically targeted intervention by God; but from a purely physical, scientific point of view it could only have been the result of some sort of highly improbable, fortuitous, random genetic mutation, the light switch of self-consciousness somehow flicked on in the animal brain by pure chance. Highly improbable, fortuitous, random, by pure chance? Well, yes and no. Self-consciousness confers amazing evolutionary advantage on any living organism that acquires it, as we can clearly see now in retrospect: being able to exert a certain degree of self-consciously intentional control over your own body and your environment immediately puts you in a different ballpark, in relation to survival, to every other non-self-conscious organism. So that, given all the evolutionary pressure, to innovate to survive, ever pushing it from behind, life—which, as we saw in the last chapter, starts out its career as pure agency, a raw, blind, non-conscious will to survive—was always going to find a way to wake up to itself one day, eventually, sooner or later, as sure as night follows day.

The evolutionary account, if anything, therefore, is even more compelling on the subject of self-consciousness than the biblical story—no surprises there, of course, because the biblical story is not literally true! But let's reflect for a moment on why the ancients insisted on interpreting all the most important things in human existence in terms of the action of the gods or God. We are back in Chapter 2 now, where we saw that the natural thing to do, in lieu of a yet to be developed detailed knowledge of physical causation, is interpret things which happen in terms of the action of invisible supernatural agencies, gods, spirits, angels, demons and so on. So that as we reflected on our own seemingly superior invisible capabilities—our intelligence, our ability to outsmart, tame and domesticate other creatures, for example—we would have seemed to ourselves to be, at least in some degree, god-like, god-chosen.

But something else was always going on, in parallel with this, as we now need to keep remembering and taking into account: the God whom we've recently realized actually exists must, somehow, all along, have been revealing things to us. There is a clear sense of this in the remarkable words of St Paul:

> For since the creation of the world God's invisible qualities—his eternal power and divine nature—have been clearly seen, being understood from what has been made, so that people are without excuse.[6]

It is a beautiful oxymoron: invisible qualities we can clearly see! Paul is talking about what is known in Christian theology as general or natural revelation.[7] We have no excuse, he admonishes, we cannot claim to have never had any sense of God's real existence, we cannot get ourselves off the hook by just saying, casually, 'Oh, I just don't believe in God.'

No excuse. This is the psychological necessity we have already contemplated, that powerful, compelling emotional push/pull that besets us all. Thus, our desperate sense of disconnection (the push) sends us ever spinning off in search of reconnection, with others, the world, the cosmos, a God we want to exist; but we wouldn't bother, would not feel any compulsion to do so, if there wasn't a real God out there already, making themself invisibly obvious, to reconnect to (the pull). If there wasn't a real God out there already? Well, surely it would then just be YOLO: eat, drink and be merry, for tomorrow we die![8] Or not even that—there would just be the desperation, the despair, unrelieved and unrelievable.

No excuse, Paul admonishes: you get the feeling he is warming us up for sin, for Original Sin. He sure is. This search for reconnection—love is the word we're looking for—is fundamentally problematic: we just do not know how (to truly love), and at this point, at any rate, we

---

6. Rom 1:20 (NIV).
7. As opposed to *special* revelation, which is the Scriptures, and, ultimately, Jesus Christ, the *Logos* (*cf* Chapter 3).
8. YOLO: You Only Live Once. 'Eat drink and be merry . . .': Eccles 8:15, Isa 22:13, I Cor 15:32.

are only interested in getting it (love)—the thought of giving it has not even occurred to us yet. Thus, the original, formative experience of self-consciousness, as we start to emerge out of Jung's mist, has us basking, even if it is just for a fleeting moment, in the absolute love and assurance of the cosmos—no doubt as a result of an outpouring, or even just a certain amount, of the unconditional regard of our parents, or of someone else who has just popped into our lives at a certain time. It has a profound effect on us—forever!

I have got to get myself some more of that, we immediately think; I have to control it, make sure it keeps coming—and this natural desire is, moreover, amplified and made all the more urgent and desperate because in the very act of becoming conscious of it we step back into the mist and lose it. Control it, make sure it keeps coming; control the world, control people; control, control, control . . . Hmmm: sin, I think you mean. For what else is sin but the attempt—futile, as it turns out—to control, manipulate, force my various relationships with others and the world, to get them and it to do what I want, to love me, to cater to my every psychological whim and fetish? Which brings us now, of course, back to the story, to the Garden, to our looming, inevitable downfall.

> Now the Lord God had planted a garden in the east, in Eden; and there he put the man he had formed. And the Lord God made all kinds of trees grow out of the ground—trees that were pleasing to the eye and good for food. In the middle of the garden were the tree of life and the tree of knowledge of good and evil.
> A river watering the garden flowed from Eden . . .[9]

Inevitable downfall? Maybe, maybe not. In the Garden story, as it unfolds in Genesis 2–3, there is no obvious time frame: how much time elapses between the establishment of the Garden as described above (2:8–10) and the temptation (3:1)? There is no telling. It could have been a matter of days, or of aeons. But the longer time goes on, the probability increases—I guess there is a sort of inevitability in that. Otherwise, there is nothing to indicate that it had to happen. It mightn't have happened; the serpent might not have turned up, we might have said 'no' anyway; we might have stayed, and still be, in the

---

9. Gen 2:8–10a (NIV).

Garden. From that purely hypothetical standpoint, God's subsequent actions in the biblical narrative to reverse the downfall would have to be considered Plan B. The bottom line, however, is that it did happen (the downfall)—and really, placing *that* tree right there in the middle of the Garden (verse 9), then expressly forbidding Eve and Adam to eat its fruit?—well, it was a bit too obvious, wasn't it?!

Remember that the writers of Genesis were, as I keep repeating myself, trying to work out what had gone wrong, were distilling the collective wisdom of countless generations before them, were being guided along the way, to boot, we must now assume, by the God who really exists, in all their invisible obviousness. The hypothesis of a primordial, original couple was, in lieu of only relatively recently elucidated compelling scientific evidence to the contrary, an entirely reasonable one. In fact, at this point in human history, the only reasonable one. I've said this before: life begets life, living things don't spring up spontaneously out of inanimate matter, they are products, with no known exception, of the creative activity of parent organisms. So, Eve and Adam were the hypothetical original parents of us all, the ancients very reasonably surmised. Where did Adam and Eve themselves come from? Well, OK, some abiogenesis there, presumably, God-fashioned from the dust (2:7)—surely a plausible explanation at the time?

Sin begetting sin too: it would have seemed the curse of every generation, from time beyond memory. This amazing propensity, quintessentially natural, for stuffing things up. Paul, again, captures the essence of the dilemma upon whose horns we seem ever to be impaled:

> I do not understand what I do. For what I want to do I do not do, but what I hate I do . . . For I know that good itself does not dwell in me, that is, in my sinful nature. For I have the desire to do what is good, but I cannot carry it out. For I do not do the good I want to do, but the evil I do not want to do—this I keep on doing. Now if I do what I do not want to do, it is no longer I who do it, but it is sin living in me that does it.[10]

'Sin living in me', like it has a life of its own, a parasitic life, imprisoning, enslaving, controlling me. It is almost like I am not really responsible

---

10. Rom 7:15–20 (NIV).

for it, it is not my fault, just something I have inherited, a congenital deformity, an addiction, not really sin, just a condition. That is the weakness, in fact, as we will see now, of the Garden story's explanation for our downfall—or maybe we've always just misunderstood, misinterpreted the story?

So, along comes the serpent: 'Did God really say . . .?'[11] Adam and Eve were in that state I described above—basking innocently in the love and assurance of the cosmos—before the nemesis came along. Well, not really. You see, the serpent (we will address the question of who exactly they were shortly) was contradicting something that had previously been said, that God had said to our beloved ancestor couple, the prohibition of eating the fruit of the tree in question:

> And the Lord God commanded the man, You are free to eat from any tree in the garden; but you must not eat from the tree of the knowledge of good and evil, for when you eat from it you will certainly die.[12]

So, they were not innocent at that point, God himself had already taken away their innocence, it was God themself who first tempted Adam and Eve, not the serpent. It was God themself who, as we suspected, very obviously, very temptingly, placed the Tree of Knowledge of Good and Evil (along with the other tree, which we'll have to account for too, eventually) right under Adam's and Eve's noses in the middle of the Garden, and compounded the artifice by drawing explicit attention to the off-limitsness of its fruit.

We always get muddled when we take these stories literally; miss the essential point, fail to notice the devil in the detail. Temptation, test, trial. What the ancients sensed, I hazard, was an amazing, essential temptation, test, trial that humans very naturally go through, that we all go through; that life, the cosmos, God puts us through. Adam and Eve are us, therefore. We don't inherit sin from them, there is no sin gene, no stain on our newborn souls; rather we recapitulate, repeat their failure of the test, somehow, inevitably, actually. We all do it individually, we are individually responsible; yes, we are. But no, we aren't, we don't do it individually, we are essentially relational,

---

11. Gen 3:1 (NIV).
12. Gen 2:16–17 (NIV).

collective, cultural creatures; we sin together—that is the sense in which it is inherited, and that, by the way, is who the serpent is.

Who the serpent is? We are born in sin, but the sin is outside us, not inside. We are born into a culture of sin-created evil; the serpent, AKA the devil, *is* that culture; the reification, the hypostatization, the personification of that culture. It is outside of us, always pre-exists us, we cannot avoid being born into it. God knows this, and rather than hide it from us they exposes us to it, throw us off the deep end into its chill waters, because they already have the solution for it—the Plan A solution for it (not Plan B after all). Knowledge of Good and Evil— AKA self-consciousness (the *imago*) and, what amounts to the same thing, moral conscience. The solution? Well, not the whole solution yet, as we'll see, but the beginning of it.

The sin is outside us, not inside? Well, yes and no. There is no doubt we inherit all sorts of genetic traits from our particular parents (thank you mummy and daddy), many or some of which might predispose us to certain types of problematic or pathological behaviour; but even were we born miraculously with no such inherited traits, the culture of sin and evil outside of us would still be there to tantalise and tempt us. At any rate, any negative traits we did have the misfortune of inheriting would still require the impact of culture outside to become actual sin.

Yes, God is tricky! 'You must not eat from the tree of knowledge of good and evil' (2:17)—amazing reverse psychology—not a prohibition but an invitation: 'Eat, eat your fill, you're going to need its nourishment for the long journey ahead.' The only way ahead is forward, no going back to the Garden, to the protective playpen of your childhood, to the womb you and all humanity were born from. Forward, as we'll see—the subject of the final chapters of this book— to the *Kingdom*; to adulthood, maturity, death, transcendence. Plan A; no Plan B.

Well, there is the antidote for the fruit's poison that will need to be administered first before we can get to the Kingdom bit, a course of treatment that may take a few or a hundred thousand years to reach its climax—we will get to all that in the next chapter. But, yes, the story is now starting to make sense—the reason why *that* tree was placed precisely in the middle of the garden with a sign on it that effectively said, 'eat me', the reason why *that* tree existed in the first place (and we haven't even got to the other tree yet). So, let's now see in exactly what way we are all Adams and Eves and somehow find ourselves, each one of us, inevitably, actually, recapitulating their failure, their fall.

We have already seen parts of the puzzle before. Human babies are born with a natural, unconscious self-absorption and self-centredness—even when they first start opening their eyes, it's obvious they are somehow not quite *there* yet. At this point in their career, they are as incapable as any non-human animal of anything but completely self-focussed behaviour. It is a state of pure, unconscious innocence.

O Botticelli angel! But it doesn't last long, as we all know. Sin begins? Not really—yet. Human babies are not non-human animals, they are born with the amazing capacity for self-consciousness, and I have claimed that you can see it (self-consciousness) flickering in the eyes of even the tiniest baby, in a way that you never see it in the eyes of a cat or a dog or a crocodile. With self-consciousness all the fun begins.

These are the two base elements—natural-born self-centredness and emerging self-consciousness—that any human child's parents, that the world and all it has got, have to contend with. This contention, for each one of us born into the world, is as urgent and dramatic as the Garden story depicts. Everything hangs on it, as we noted at the start of our story, everything from peace and harmony in the school playground to global peace and harmony.

The Garden is the protective matrix of its parents' unconditional love the child is innocently born into—at least in theory. God is the parents—obviously! It is a walled garden of that part of the world, the Middle East, a paradise, an oasis, a place of perfect security, predictability, and happiness. Outside the garden is the treacherous, hostile desert, no water, just danger, wild animals, marauding invaders. But, no, it is also the land, the life, of opportunity, of adulthood and making your own way in the world; a land and life that cannot be avoided, that has to be faced, that is always the future of our lives. It is dangerous and scary—at least that is what your parents might warn you of early on—but from your state of secure, protected innocence your parents' warnings ring hollow, you do not believe them—their entreaties and admonitions only serve to highlight the tantalizing possibilities.

Parenthood: it is such a tricky, uncertain, divided thing. On one hand you need to protect your child from the world, on the other to prepare them for it. It is so easy to stuff up, almost impossible to get completely right, or even half right. The world threatens, but it also promises, and, at any rate, you cannot hide it from your child forever. So, your task is to gradually train your little darling up for it, even knowing you can never do so perfectly and that there are many things, even the most important things, your child will just have to work out for themselves. Even knowing that one day you will just have to chuck them out of the nest to fly for themselves—knowing how much that will hurt you and terrify you but how necessary it is for you to do so—knowing that it could all turn out disastrously, that your child might end up a complete failure or even a seriously bad person. Knowing that you will always, somehow, be there for them regardless, but that the essential self-conscious freedom they are born with, born to, is the most precious, vital thing of all, and that it requires you to gradually, sooner or later, necessarily, let them go.

We are talking about a good parent, a wise parent, the best sort of parent. About God, in other words, the imagined ideal parent—whom, as you know, by the way, we have recently decided is not just an imagined ideal, but actually exists. None of us can ever live up to such an ideal, but we try. In fact, as we work out sooner or later, our only hope in being a good or a great, or even just an adequate parent, is in realising we need outside help. We commonly look to the example and assistance of our own parents for this, and to the community and culture around us for support and encouragement. But there's the rub again: our parents might have tried hard themselves but just not been very good at it, our community and culture might likewise be full of flaws and pathologies in relation to parenting. And, at any rate, there may be some people in our communities who go into parenting without the best of intentions, without the slightest idea, or even interest, in being a good parent.

So, yes, the whole process is fraught with peril—but the potential reward, the outcome of the child as a great or at least half-decent adult human being, makes parenting well and truly a risk worth taking—apart from being critical for the future of the human race and the planet anyway, as we noted at the outset of our tale. It is clear, however, in relation to humanity as a whole, that outside help is needed, beyond our own parents, beyond human culture, otherwise we have no chance. What we need, therefore (here I go repeating myself again) is an ideal parent—an Ur-Parent, an Über-Parent—to look to. The God Who Exists, in other words.

What most essentially does the child need to know? Well, as we have been saying, human life is uniquely driven by not one but two necessities: physical and psychological. So, parents are faced with the task of training their little protégés, firstly, to be able to 'take care of number one', which includes everything from being able to dress themselves and kick the footy, to being able to work hard, make sacrifices, save up to buy a house. Simultaneously there's the other thing: the protégés need to learn how to get on with people.

Two necessities, not one, uniquely for humans because of the *imago dei*, self-consciousness. How to get on with people: how to cooperate creatively with others in family, friendships, community, society. As we've noted repeatedly, some non-zero modicum of selflessness, of care, consideration and respect for others and for all things, is the essential, vital element. But the starting point for learning selflessness is knowing the difference between selfishness and selflessness—knowing when we are being bad, or evil, and when we are being good. If we cannot tell the difference, there's no hope for us at all, no possibility of ever escaping from our natural narcissism.

Moral conscience, in other words. In the biblical story it is what we get by eating the fruit of *that* tree. Something we do not get if we do not eat, if Eve and Adam did not eat back in the day. We would be stuck still in the Garden today, well and truly bored out of our brains, stuck in an eternal infantile childhood. Help! Get me out of here! Thank you, Eve, thank you, Adam, for eating that fruit!

How does it work in our own childhood? Our parents are God, on one hand, though a flawed version thereof: they mediate God's love and care into our lives, acting, essentially, *in loco dei*, you might say, *in place of God*. The serpent on the other hand, as I have said, is the culture of sin we are born into and which impinges on us probably from even before we pop out of the womb, constantly tempting us to be selfish, to think only of number one, to just go for what we want regardless of the feelings, needs or wants of anyone or everyone else. How is this serpentine culture mediated into our lives? Well—surprise, surprise—it is mediated primarily, at least early on, by who else but our parents, with their own flaws, weaknesses, sinfulness? So, our parents are also *in loco diaboli—in place of the devil*! Both God *and* serpent, our beloved mater and pater.

'Constantly tempting us to be selfish, to think only of number one . . .'—sounds pretty familiar, I think you will agree. Temptation to sin, evil, is not the sole content of human culture, of course, which has all sorts of good things in it as well—albeit only by courtesy of previous outside interventions from the God of love, you are probably expecting me to say—but it is the part of it that tempts us, that appeals to our natural born self-centredness, as we begin to wake up and become conscious of ourselves, our desires and abilities. Parents of little children fight these battles every day, and we are almost always conflicted in it. Am I being too hard, or too soft? Am I being hypocritical—where could they have got that annoying little selfish behaviour pattern from, other than from me? I cannot keep shielding them and protecting them from their own foolishness and selfishness forever, someday they're going to have to face the consequences themselves and learn the hard way.

You have a sense of God's confliction too as the Hebrew Old Testament unfolds post-Garden. He is a gentle, gracious god of love who rains down blessings on his people one minute, but the next he's raining down fire and brimstone and judgement—mercifully saving Lot and his family from the destruction of Sodom and Gomorrah, then turning the man's poor wife into a pillar of salt just because she looks back while fleeing the conflagration.[13] Don't look back, whatever you do!

These are stories that shocked us all when we were growing up and might have fuelled our atheist tendencies. What good is a conflicted God?—it would be better if there was no god at all. And there is not; but no there is! Of course, the apparent confliction is all our own, reflected in the mirror of heaven. God seems to finally get their act together when they incarnate as Jesus, who then takes all our sins and suffering upon himself to the Cross—no conflict in sight or even possible at this point, just perfect self-sacrifice, pain and death.

More on that (God getting their act together) in the next chapter. In the Garden story God is not a flawed, conflicted human parent but the perfect, ideal parent of all humanity, so the temptation appears to come from a third-party source. I say 'appears' because the serpent is not a genuine supernatural rival to God but a created being like the rest of us, so they can only get at Eve and Adam if God gives them

---

13. Gen 19.

permission; and, seeing that God, as we have suggested, is the one who started the whole temptation ball rolling in the first place, you would have to say that it is more than just permission that the serpent got, more like active instigation, more like co-conspirator status—another sense in which our own human, non-divine parents act in place of both God and devil.

Now, the serpent, what did he say? Well, he:

> ... said to the woman, 'Did God really say, "You must not eat from any tree in the garden" ... 'You will not certainly die ... For God knows that when you eat from it your eyes will be opened, and you will be like God, knowing good and evil' [3:1–5].

This is the strange, inexplicable way in which our parents tempt us, cannot help but do so, find themselves compelled to do so by a profound inner compulsion. On one hand they conscientiously lay down the law, train us to say please and thank you, confront our wilful self-centredness with injunctions to be considerate towards others, take turns, play nicely, share—the fruit, no doubt, of their own parents' hard labours in them, of the God of love in all humanity. On the other, the serpent inside them compels them to project their own wilful self-centredness onto their beloved child, to wish for them to be cool, admired, successful, better at stuff than other kids, better looking, a winner not a loser. Our children become extensions of our own ego, and we (we are the parents now) find ourselves living our own lives through them, becoming the worst of parents—controlling, 'helicopter' parents, spoiling their children till they are rotten—until or unless we become aware of what we're doing and pull out of the death spiral before it's too late.

'Did God really say ...? ...You will not certainly die ... You will be like God.' 'Like God': yes, like God in knowing good and evil—that is the good part of it, the essential thing we need, a moral conscience, the very thing that will save our lives every day of the week in adult life—the very thing without which everyone will hate us, spurn us, probably wish us to die of causes unnatural if not natural. But the serpent also means 'like God' in the sense of having power and control of our own lives on a par with God, in a way that makes God unnecessary, redundant—we can do just as well without you God, without following your rules, thank you very much. Even more than this: we can do *better* without you, we can be gods ourselves, you are now officially out of a job. And, oh, by the way, I don't think you even exist anymore—no, in fact you definitely don't!

You can see that this is where it really all begins—atheism I mean. 'By the way, I don't believe in God': what we mean when we say this is not mere intellectual dissent, it is a declaration of independence: 'Even if you do exist I don't need you, I don't particularly trust you anyway—you lied to me, you said I would die if I ate the fruit but I didn't—I don't need to trust you, I trust myself, I can do better without you, thank you very much—and oh, by the way, come to think of it, now that I recall, you don't exist anyway and never did.' Atheism: it is not so much that we don't believe in God, as don't trust in, have faith in, actually need God. Who cares if God exists?!—and oh, by the way, you definitely do not, never did.

It is no coincidence that we talk to the God who doesn't exist in the same defiant way we sometimes talk to our parents. But this is only the sin side of the coin; in our moments of defiance, we simultaneously experience a pang of conscience—or at least we do if our parents haven't abrogated the God side of their parental calling altogether. Some children do roll on into adult life with little or no moral conscience, but, fortunately, this rarely happens. Why? Because Eve and Adam actually ate the fruit—did not abrogate their part in God's plan and defy the serpent instead. Once again: thank you, oh our primordial parents!

Well, thank you, oh our own parents, I should say, seeing Adam and Eve never actually existed. We cannot stay in the protective matrix of our parents' love forever; any more than our non-existent primordial forebears could have stayed in the Garden forever. It is something about being born in *imago dei*, with the innate capacity for self-consciousness—everything about it in fact. The serpent didn't bother trying to tempt any non-human animals, God did not prohibit anyone but humans from eating the tree's fruit. Only human animals have the capacity to defy their parents, be selfish, know good and evil, develop a moral conscience, set out on the road towards becoming a good or an evil adult human animal.

A horrifying image of my childhood was a photograph in a nature book of a lion tucking into a wildebeest, seemingly still alive—the violent evil of the lion, the innocent victimhood of the wildebeest. But, no, as I reflect now, the lion was just doing its thing, the wildebeest its, no horror or tragedy intended. Another image that scarred me was in a footy book, burly Richmond ruckman, Captain Blood Jack Dyer, caught in the brutal act of punching a little St Kilda rover whose name has long since escaped my memory—in this case, yes, real horror, real sin!

Self-consciousness: what Eve and Adam immediately experienced upon eating the fruit. Their eyes were opened, and they saw, for the first time, that they were naked—despite having walked around in their birthday suits since time immemorial. Self-consciousness, embarrassment, shame. Little children obliviously walk around butt-naked, which charms everyone, until the day they never do it again, having been gradually trained to cover up by their parents. We become self-conscious, conscious of ourselves as selves, and, yes, it can be pretty embarrassing!

It is the next bit of the Garden story, God's radical response to Adam and Eve's newly realized self-consciousness, that has us now grasping for an explanation, however:

> And the Lord God said, 'The man has now become like one of us, knowing good and evil. He must not be allowed to reach out his hand and take also from the tree of life and eat, and live forever.' So the Lord God banished him from the Garden of Eden to work the ground from which he had been taken. After he drove the man out, he placed on the east side of the Garden of Eden cherubim and a flaming sword flashing back and forth to guard the way to the tree of life.[14]

They did not die, as God predicted then the serpent contradicted.[15] But yes they did. For unknown, timeless aeons Adam and Eve had been wandering around the Garden naked in blissful innocence. The clock of time had not started yet, they did not age, they did not grow up or grow old. But now, with the disobedient eating of the fruit, the curse of time, which leads only to death, began in earnest. Curses: pain in childbirth for every woman; infertility and intractability of

---

14. Gen 3:22–24.
15. Gen 2: [16] And the Lord God commanded the man, 'You are free to eat from any tree in the garden; [17] but you must not eat from the tree of the knowledge of good and evil, for when you eat from it you will certainly die.' Then Gen 3: [4] 'You will not certainly die', the serpent said to the woman.

the soil and of plant life; the necessity of hard, back-breaking work, physical death itself inevitably.[16]

Physical death inevitably: 'until you return to the ground, since from it you were taken.' Why do I say, *physical* death? Is there some other sort of death? Well, yes. Remember, the Garden story didn't happen, there were no actual curses, no Adam and Eve to curse. Physical death—the sooner or later expiry of organic bodies, every last one of them/us—has been around since the beginning of life on earth, it seems to be an essential property of life itself, it certainly doesn't start with humans.

Don't take it literally—as we keep saying! It is really another sort of death, a much more profound and significant death, that the story must be trying to get at—even if the biblical writers, at the time, depicted it as physical death, and presumably understood it solely in those terms. Eve and Adam are summarily dismissed from the Garden, never able to return, lest they partake of the antidote to this other sort of death.

A psychological, you might even say spiritual, death. Separation from God, eternal spiritual separation from God. That is what expulsion from the Garden symbolises. Ah, that is why we cannot find God anywhere, now, outside the Garden; that is why I am an atheist, why God doesn't seem to exist. It's their fault, they have only got themselves to blame that we don't believe in them anymore. We might want 'to get ourselves back to the Garden',[17] as Joni Mitchell sings, but there is no going back, no Garden to go back to—by all accounts, as far as we can tell, it must have been shut down altogether after Eve and Adam's departure.

Separation from God. Expulsion from the Garden. The dawn of atheism. This is Plan A, remember. We (humans) were made for the big wide world outside, the Garden is the protective matrix of our parents' love, *in loco dei*, in our childhood and youth; now we have grown up, left home before or when our parents booted us out, and are making our own way in the world. There is always no other way. Yes, something inside of us dies, but only that we be born again at the next level.

---

16. Gen 2:16–19.
17. 'We are stardust, we are golden, and we have got to get ourselves back to the Garden.' Joni Mitchell, *Woodstock*, 1970.

This is the obvious content of coming-of-age initiation rites in traditional societies the world over, which typically involve some sort of ritual, simulated separation (from parents and tribe) and dying.[18] The 'death of innocence' might be a poetic way of putting it, but it is clearly not a physical death, even when it is symbolised as such. Again, the mistake we always make is to take the story literally, as if it really was that physical death came into the world through Adam and Eve's action. The curse of physical death symbolises a death far worse, far more cataclysmic: psychological or spiritual separation from God, from our parents. That is the state we found ourselves in, find ourselves in, when we wilfully left the Garden, leave our parents.

'He must not be allowed to reach out his hand and take also from the tree of life and eat, and live forever.' You see, the possibility of living forever was a new thing, a new possibility opened up by Eve and Adam's God/serpent inspired choice. Danger, danger, danger, however. Humans are not yet ready for forever living. Expulsion from the Garden is no punishment for our primordial ancestors, rather it is their salvation, or at least the beginning of it. Salvation from the danger, the potential disaster of eating the fruit of the tree of life before we're ready. The potential disaster is living forever, but in permanent eternal separation from God, eternal self-exile. *Hell*, in other words!

Hells bells! Literally, in fact. I'm running ahead by talking about hell and salvation; that's the topic of the next chapter. But the loss of any sense or fear of hell and of a spiritual death far more awful than mere physical death is a central component of the atheism of our present age, a key part of its danger, danger, danger. Something far worse than human extinction or even the physical end of all life on earth.

The thought, the idea of hell: the mother/father of all panic attacks. The Garden expulsion is in real time, it's where time begins. So, the spiritual separation, death, hell it prefigures must be in real time. Right now, in fact. Mostly we are oblivious to it; but if you have ever had an actual, real, live panic attack, you will know exactly what I mean. You know logically that you are not going to (physically, actually) die, but you fear something far worse—never being able to escape from the

---

18. Exclusion and dying may also be simulated by acts such as, for example, circumcision, scarification, removal of a tooth or a part of a finger, which also serve to identify initiates with their new life as an adult.

feeling of panic—not even, or especially not, by doing something like killing yourself. A feeling, a state of mind, a psychological, spiritual state of eternal, never-ever escape from anxiety and fear, from panic. Hell in other words—eternal separation from being able to live as a normal person in the world, eternal psychological and spiritual separation from all other selves, alone, cooped up inside your own head forever. Not even suicide can save you; suicide would just clinch the deal, permanently cut off any possible escape route.

Help! What eventually gets you out of the death-spiral, which really is the most perfect of delusions, is the amazing realization that it is a choice you are making yourself, that your hell would be your own prophecy self-fulfilled. Then you reach out to another person, one other person, almost any other person: 'Help me!' And the spell is broken. You escape back to life.

Yes, the Tree of Life, the possibility of living forever. God certainly intends us to eat of its fruit, else why would he have plonked it right there in the middle of the Garden next to that other tree? But only when we are ready, when we have learned some important things first. The question is how can we live life in a way that transcends physical death? Transcend it *now*, I mean, quite apart from any wild speculation about an afterlife to come. A greater life to come *now*, in this life; don't wait till after.

It is a state of mind, of consciousness; a spiritual state that cannot be weighed down by our resistant physicality. There is something, a type of psychological, spiritual experience that you might think of as a reverse panic attack, that might give us a sense of it. A sense, a vision not of eternal separation but eternal connection. Eternal re-connection. A euphoric drug-induced state, perhaps? A natural high? Yeah, probably. The sort of feeling of oneness with all things that people aspire to in meditative practice? Surely.

Panic attack or euphoria—maybe you've never experienced either. Our lives are lived, mostly, in the intermediate zone between mild connection—we are happy, things are going well, we are on a roll, we get on well with people, we are contented, satisfied, at peace—and mild disconnection—we feel uneasy, a bit frustrated, vaguely dissatisfied, things are a bit out of kilter, we are not having a great day. Connection: psychological necessity drives us ever on, as we have seen, searching for it, with greater or lesser degrees of desperation. But it is essentially problematic, as we've also seen. We want to be connected, to be loved, but our self-consciousness keeps getting in the way. It doesn't come naturally to us, we have to learn it—learn to be selfless, vulnerable, open; to be sources of love not just sinks. That is where our parents, and others around us in society as we are growing up, come in—that is where the God who really exists comes in.

I am repeating myself. But God knows that eating fruit from the Tree of Life before we know how to love, or have even the slightest idea of it, would be a disaster. It would give us total power, total control, not over mere physical life, but over psychological, spiritual life. Some people seem to have actually already eaten quite a lot of it—in spite of what the Garden story (literally) says. There's a beautiful of description of such a possessed creature in Dostoevsky's *Demons*, the amazing character of Stavrogin. I urge you to read the full text of Stavrogin's written confession, presented to the saintly Bishop Tikhon.[19] At a certain point Stavrogin claims:

> Every situation in my life in which I have ever happened to find myself, however unspeakably shameful, utterly degrading, vile and, most importantly, ridiculous, has always aroused both boundless anger and unbelievable pleasure in me. Precisely the same has also been true in moments when I was committing a crime, and in moments when my life was in danger. If I was stealing something, then while I was perpetrating the theft, my awareness of the depths of my vileness would send me into ecstasy. It was not vileness that I loved (here my reason remained fully intact), but rather, the ecstasy I derived from the tormenting awareness of having fallen so low that was so gratifying . . .

We have all probably had a nibble, or at least been momentarily intoxicated by the aroma, the possibility, of eating it (the fruit of *that* tree). But some seem to have, yes, engorged themselves. Such people do indeed seem evil, possessed by demons, have dark magical powers. Your average narcissist, psychopath, criminal kingpin or tyrant, for example. Need I name names?! Total, iron, vice-like control over one's own will; so compelling, so powerful, that it casts a spell over others, a

---

19. Dostoevsky, *Demons* (also known as *The Possessed*, *The Devils*), 1871–1872, Appendix: *At Tikhon's*. The chapter belongs in the middle of the book, but as later introductions note, Dostoevsky's original publisher refused to publish it at the time, insisted he omit it.

psychic spell that bends their will to yours completely. Then, in some cases, just to compound the pleasure, the control, you find yourself eating your victims—it is a psychopath's life!

Yes, eating fruit from the first tree just brings on common or garden individual sin, but the other tree's fruit spawns something that operates collectively, beyond the level or control of private individuals, namely evil. Real evil. The serpent, the devil, by the way, is, as I have said, the personification (well, snake equivalent thereof) of this thing, collective sin, evil. You could even speculate that that is who the devil, Satan, actually is: a created being who had previously eaten his fill of Tree of Life fruit and led a full-scale rebellion against God—except that we're not taking the story literally, remember!

Participation in evil: how does it work? It is not just sin, an intentional rejection of God, an incidental desire to 'do my own thing'; it is a rejection of conscience itself, a rejection out-of-hand of the fruit of the other tree, like we bypass the first lot of fruit and go straight to the second. Like Stavrogin. Such evil intentionality goes out into the world, into the collectivity, the culture, we give birth to it, spawn it as an evil child, a pathological purely virtual organism with a life of its own, far more powerful than any mere individual human. Thus, the tyrant can enslave hundreds or thousands or millions of individual minds to their cause by wielding the evil power of, for example, nationalism, racism, xenophobia—the evil, atheist spell they weave: 'There is no God, I am God, come and be gods with me . . .'

But, no, it only ever promises, threatens total control, never actually delivers. God did actually chuck us out of the Garden after all—so the story goes—did absolutely cut us off from that tree. You can smell, but you cannot eat. Thus, no-one can, actually, psychologically, totally control themselves; can never control others, psychologically, totally. Not even the fictional Stavrogin, although you will have to read the book to find out what becomes of him in the end. Hitler suicided, Stalin died of natural causes—physical life, and God, catch up with you eventually, even if you've murdered millions. Thank you, God: our wilful souls are always constrained, in the final analysis, when push comes to shove, by the intrinsic limitations of our physical bodies—no one's will, with a mere human physical brain and body as its instruments of malice, can totally control itself, let alone a bunch of others. Physical death, you might say, is an essential part of the salvation of spiritual life.

Physical death, salvation? Saved by death?... Sounds interestingly familiar, don't you think?! But now we really are running ahead. So, before we go down that road—the salvation road—in the next chapter, let's briefly recap. What exactly have we decided in this current chapter is so original about sin? Well, it is a human original, for starters, no non-human animal is capable of it. We are, uniquely, self-conscious (embarrassingly so sometimes), whether by incidental divine intervention—the *imago dei*—or, better still perhaps, by the raw inevitability of the evolutionary process; and this confers on us the ability to perform all sorts of magic tricks non-human animals cannot. But it also opens us up to the possibility, the very high probability, of sin. Yes, sin: intentionally, self-consciously doing selfish, bad things which hurt ourselves and others.

The Garden story tells it all. We are born into a world which both promises and threatens, a culture of both good and evil, our parents its gate-keeping representatives, simultaneously both nurturing gods and tempting serpents. Yes, our parents, in most cases and at least to some degree, protect us, nourish and nurture us, love us with a perfect selfless love that can only come from a source outside both themselves and culture—from the real God whom we've just recently decided necessarily exists. But this is not enough, no matter how intentional and committed to the project they are. For they will also, tempting serpents that they also are, inevitably, whether by accident or (heaven forbid) by intention, introduce us to sin. So, they need to, judiciously, at a certain point, start administering the antidote—they need to find a way to introduce their little darling to that real God, who is—no surprises—the only one who can actually, truly save them.

Darling, this is God; God, meet darling. Yes, it has to be an explicit introduction, making of acquaintance. This in fact is the subject of the next two chapters. Loving your child is not enough, no matter how bursting with unconditionality your love is. At some point every human being needs a direct infusion straight from the source—at some point the whole of humanity needs such an infusion. The ability to get on with others, to be sociable, to show some consideration, respect, to put yourself out for others every now and again; a moral conscience, a basic knowledge of right and wrong—these are necessary, but they are not sufficient. Why not? Because it is just too powerful, our propensity for sin, this culture of sin and evil we are born into. We absolutely need direct outside help.

If you don't think it—our propensity for sin, this culture of sin and evil we are born into—is powerful, then go back to the start of Chapter 1. Help! The polycrisis: human sin and selfishness now threatening the whole globe and the future of our species. That's power; that's danger, that's threat. We're addicted to sin and only a power greater than ourselves can save us.[20] But we're following God's Plan A, remember, so let us now see what that amazing deity whom we've now realized absolutely must exist had up their sleeve for us next—what plans they set in place to save us—after they unceremoniously, wise ideal parent that they are, booted us out of that lovely Garden.

---

20. AA Step 2 of 12: 'Came to believe that a Power greater than ourselves could restore us to sanity.'

Chapter 5
No Plan B

Nothing in this world, in human history, is not part of a divine plan—that is the outlandish sort of possibility you have to contemplate when you shock yourself by admitting, as we have done, that God might or even must exist. As much as it sticks in the throat, yes, I (*homo sapiens*) am not running the show, I am not alone in charge of my own destiny, I will not be the hero, the saviour, of my own life.[1] And not just any God, any plan: a God quintessentially of love, a plan to bring this unruly, ornery human species, and the world it is part of, to some sort of marvellous fruition, or at least save it from complete destruction. Apparently.

I might not be the hero, the saviour, but one human will be, or rather was, on behalf of us all, so that through us the whole world will be saved and brought to fruition. We who threaten the world with extinction also the potential saviours of it? Go figure! That, at any rate, is the unlikely story we will begin to unfold in the present chapter, although I'm sure you're already busy guessing who that one human will be, or was. Guess away.

Love is not enough, we acknowledged at the end of the last chapter. Specifically, even the best sort of selfless, unconditional love human parents can muster, off their own bat, for their child—it is not enough, on its own, to overcome the power of sin, as it beckons to the child from the culture around, calls out to the child's natural born self-centredness. More powerful medicine—more powerful love—is needed, in fact, as we also acknowledged: an explicit presentation

---

1. 'Whether I shall turn out to be the hero of my own life, or whether that station will be held by anybody else, these pages must show.' The opening sentence of *David Copperfield* by Charles Dickens [1850] (London: Penguin, 2004).

of the God of love to the child, from an early age preferably. In the Christian tradition this process typically starts with the well-known rite of infant *baptism*, in which parents act as a sort of proxy to mediate God into their child's life, then reaches its climax, if all goes according to plan, with *confirmation*, when the teenager or young adult consciously and intentionally accepts the faith of their parents for themselves, entering into confirmed membership of the church in their own right.

Many faiths and societies, traditional and modern, have, as we noted in the last chapter, corresponding coming-of-age rites and rituals which usher the young into adult life in the community. Such rites, however, provide no sure guarantee, especially in the contemporary west, where fewer and fewer young people have anything at all to do with Christianity, and even those whose parents do inflict it on them are readily sucked back out of the church by the dominant culture of atheism around them, so powerfully enticing is that culture.

The human race as a whole is in precisely the same position of vulnerability. I am speaking from an evolutionary perspective: with our unique self-consciousness, our oversized intellects and our natural self-centredness, we would surely have wiped ourselves off the face of the earth long ago had we been left to our own devices. Somehow, in some way, as a matter of evolutionary necessity, we have to learn to live together cooperatively in families, communities, societies, avoiding the sort of conflict that can lead to mutual destruction; so, as we've seen, we have always needed and still need a teacher outside ourselves, a God of love intervening from outside human culture and history, to show us the way. Let us now take up the story of this ongoing intervention from where we left off last chapter. As it turns out, only a very explicit presentation indeed, of God to the child, will, historically speaking, finally clinch the deal.

> And the Lord God said, 'The man has now become like one of us, knowing good and evil. He must not be allowed to reach out his hand and take also from the tree of life and eat, and live forever.' So the Lord God banished him from the Garden of Eden to work the ground from which he had been taken.[2]

---

2. Gen 3:22–23 (NIV).

With expulsion from the Garden history begins, as we have seen, so we will need now to start taking the text more literally. It was (the expulsion) for our own good, evidently, as we've realized, the consequences of eating from the Tree of Life as well, straight away, too terrifying to risk: spiritual death, eternal separation from God, eternal self-entrapment in the closed, vicious circle of our own minds, actual hell.

A fate, you might say, far worse than (physical) death. So, what do we do now? Very quickly we need to set about the task of learning how to live together, creatively and harmoniously, in community, so we can avoid self-destruction. To do so we need to acquire, by whatever means possible, the capacity for at least an occasional bit of selflessness. The Hebrew Bible, as humans leave the Garden and start to spread out around the globe, tracks the trials and tribulations of one particular human group, the ancient Hebrews or Israelites, now known as Jews, going down that road. The Jewish people—and, now, all Christians and Muslims—trace their origins back to one historical figure, the great patriarch Abraham.

We first meet Abraham—at this point called just Abram—in Chapter 12 of the book of Genesis, when God calls him to leave the land of his birth, Ur of the Chaldeans, in ancient Mesopotamia, modern day Iraq. This is around 1800 BCE according to Jewish tradition. To leave, to migrate with his whole household, to 'a land I will show you', a 'promised land', to 'the land of Canaan'—modern day Palestine/Israel and parts of surrounding territories.

What for, exactly—this perilous journey to an unknown land on the whim of an invisible deity? God tells Abram:

> I will make you into a great nation, and I will bless you; I will make your name great, and you will be a blessing. I will bless those who bless you, and whoever curses you I will curse; and all peoples on earth will be blessed through you.[3]

At first you think, that's nice for Abraham—'I will make *you* into a great nation, and I will bless *you*'—but what about the other poor saps around, the entire rest of the human race? It seems exclusive, partial, a God who has favourites. Yes, the apparent chosenness of Abraham and his descendants, any sense of Jewish exceptionalism, and even, later, Christian exceptionalism, immediately gets your hackles up,

---

3. Gen 12:2–3 (NIV).

and rightly so, but don't let that make you then miss or misinterpret the punchline, the goal of God's great plan: 'all peoples on earth will be blessed through you.' Ah, the greatness of Abraham and his descendants will not be actually in their own right, but as a seed, a messenger people, a pilot-project, through which the whole world will eventually be blessed. That was the intention, the purpose—even if, as it turned out, they often deviated from the path and, usually unsuccessfully, sought greatness in their own right.

Blessed in what way, great in what way? God's plan, God's purpose, is, as we have anticipated, to save the human race—specifically, to teach us how to overcome our natural self-centredness so that we can learn the art of living together in positive and creative ways. By the time we get to Abraham's famous descendant Moses, about 400 years later, we realise that God has a literal plan, of how a great community or society could operate, ready to unfurl—we'll get to that shortly. But why choose Abraham to be the founding father of the great pilot-project? Because somehow, he was the only good or righteous person around at the time who could be trusted with such a task? Certainly not: it is Abraham's faith, his trust, his crazy, seemingly blind obedience to God's instructions and commands, as we read the remainder of his life story (Genesis 12–25), rather than any personal goodness or righteousness, that stands out and stands to his credit. Blind faith in an invisible deity—yeah, that's something you really have to admire!

The proof of the pudding, the pilot-project, will be in the eating, at any rate—we will get to the Mosaic covenant shortly, and eventually to the so-called 'Kingdom' and modern democracy. But at this point faith in and obedience to an invisible deity—one who really exists and moreover well and truly has the best interests of humanity in their sights—is the key. Sure, Abraham does seem a bit crazy, listening to a voice coming out of the sky—I recommend you watch the 1966 religious epic *The Bible . . . In the Beginning*, with an exasperated Abraham/George C Scott receiving instructions from a disembodied voice sounding suspiciously like director John Huston's, to get a sense of the sheer nuttiness of it.[4] But just this sort of nuttiness turns out to be the game-changer for humanity.

---

4. *The Bible . . . In the Beginning* (1966), produced by Dino De Laurentiis, directed by John Huston.

Faith in an invisible God whose voice we hear in our imagination—it is the time-honoured formula of religious believers the world-over, calculated to infuriate and invite the contempt of every card-carrying non-believer! Genesis records at least seven times when God, allegedly, speaks directly to Abraham, each time renewing his acquaintance, giving him specific instructions and reassuring him of their (God's) commitment to the overall deal to make him (Abraham) into a great nation. Why does Abraham hear from God so much? Because he's open to hearing from them (God), he wants to hear from them, he's desperate to hear from them. Having heard once—the thrill of it, the amazing sense of purpose and destiny it gives, the hope, the fulfillment it delivers—you just want more, can never get enough of it.

It is a practised ear, an active listening, any true believer will explain. Yes, a voice inside your head, although it often seems so only in retrospect; a voice imagined, not literally audible, despite its dramatized depictions in film; a voice mediated by our imagination and by the culture outside of us, as we saw in Chapter 2 and 3. A voice whose proof of veracity is in the eating of the pudding of your life: is it sweet, and fruitful, does obedience to it bear fruit? If not, then maybe you are just hearing things!

A voice, moreover, you can only hear—frustratingly so, for sure—if you have faith. There is a serious Catch-22 here: you can't hear the voice of the invisible God without faith, but how can you have faith without hearing from and experiencing that God in the first place?! Faith is enigmatic, paradoxical. But it is also very simple, the simplest thing. Where do we first come across it, each of us, in our own lives? In the amazing faith and trust little children have in their parents, blinded, dazzled by all that unconditional love pouring into them, all that faithfulness and trustworthiness. Or not, as the case may be: you can readily see here a profound way faith can be lost, or never kindled in the first place, the opposite of faith kindled instead, anxiety of the deepest kind.

Little Abram growing up in Mesopotamia 3800 years ago, in his parents' house, in the bosom of his parents' unconditional love, faithfulness, trustworthiness; his faith and trust growing. Sometime later, all grown up and with a family of his own, having followed his now dead father Terah as far as Haran (perhaps in modern day southern Turkey), he turns his back on the past completely and departs, for good, to parts unknown. Go figure?! Why does he go? The call of the wild, the thirst for adventure, the sort of deep, compelling inner urge that has inspired humans throughout history to flee, to migrate, to escape poverty and insecurity, to seek freedom and greener pastures in the wide blue yonder on the other side? All or any of these, surely. And not just freedom and greener pastures for himself, but for his family, his children, his children's children, countless generations into the future—that is real selflessness, caring for a countless bunch of other selves who don't even exist yet! The sort of real selflessness only obedience to the call of an invisible God in whom he, Abraham, has absolute faith and trust can deliver.

Something amazing must have happened, evidently, in between his parents' compound in Ur and his departure for the promised land. Something amazing happens to us as well, for we likewise, at a certain point, sooner or later, leave our parents' house, the protective matrix of our parents' love, and heed the call of the wild. It is not, in either case, ideally, or at least usually, a breakdown of trust in our parents, rather a transformation of it. Do we learn to trust in ourselves, perchance, becoming independent and no longer needing our parents? Well, yes and no. Think about Abraham. No doubt he had already acquired substantial independent life skills and considerable means of his own prior to the call from God—after all, he was by all accounts a young seventy-five by the time he finally struck out on his own.[5] But no, far more than trusting his own abilities, he trusted a much greater power, invisible, outside—way outside—of himself.

Yes, presumably there was, as is the case of refugee and migrant peoples throughout history, political, social and economic pressure on Abraham to make the big move. No doubt, in fact: God's promise, God's plan, is always for a better, a greater, a truer life. In our own case, always our parents wish for us, always we seek, a better life, true freedom, true fulfillment. The transformation of our childhood faith in our parents is, when it works ideally, an expansion of that faith to trust in community, society, the world, life itself—which includes faith and trust in ourselves, of course. Not merely an expansion, however, for making the quantum leap to trusting in the world, the cosmos, in life in general, and thus truly in ourselves, involves just that, a quantum leap. Grown up faith in the world, in life itself, is different in kind, not just degree, to childhood faith in parents.

---

5. Gen 12:4.

Abraham made the leap, very consciously and intentionally in fact, the fruit, presumably, of his parents' explicit introduction to him, from an early age, of the loving, invisible God who, as we now know, truly exists. Little children as a rule respond very readily to such introductions, as we will see shortly. But there is no other possible explanation for Abraham's remarkable faith, even if he eventually took it to a level well beyond that of his parents and the rest of his family, a quite remarkable level for any human of the time, or any time, perhaps. In our own case, even though some amount of such generalised faith is essential to being able to leave home at all, mostly we are not nearly so conscious and intentional about it. We muddle through life, making the best of our abilities and limitations, and many of us are beset by worries and anxieties of various kinds, which are more or less debilitating—gaps or holes in our faith and trust in the world, a faith and trust that is, in the final analysis, just a limited expansion of our childhood faith in our parents, not a leap across a gap; or maybe we had no such faith in our parents in the first place anyway?

Lately we have been worrying that the world is coming to an end, that our species might extinguish itself. Or we are beset with fears over the rising cost of living, our job security, our children's participation in school. Anxiety, by all indicators, is rampant, along with depression, post-traumatic stress; people suffer panic attacks and breakdowns, seek medicine and therapy—and I am not just talking about people in Ukraine or Israel/Palestine or Yemen! Anxiety and its variants are, yes, all antonyms of faith, trust. Abraham lived in a world that was, almost certainly, significantly more hostile, dangerous, uncertain than the world most of us live in today, yet rather than being paralysed by fear he was energized by faith.

Faith, then, is the key. Faith in an invisible God who somehow, nevertheless, exists, and, moreover, is all-powerful and loves you to bits. Such faith is inexplicable to us adults who have not been explicitly introduced to this God in childhood. You might have some greater or lesser degree of faith in yourself, you might trust to some degree the social institutions and culture around you—or not, depending on where you live right now—you must have some sort of faith or trust in something just to get you out of bed in the morning, to stop you from grinding to a halt, from descending into apathy or despair, even ending it all. But faith or trust in the abstract, in the infinite or universal, in the invisible? You've got to be kidding. Faith in—precisely—nothing?!

Well, Abraham had plenty of it—faith in an abstract, universal nothing—more than most, probably, we've suggested. Little children, in contrast to most modern adults, also have no trouble with the idea of it, when parents diligently introduce it to them from early childhood. As we saw in Chapter 2, they happily imagine and relate to animals or train engines or clouds that smile and talk and behave like humans, none of whom, obviously, they can literally see; so why not an invisible deity, an invisible nothing, whom they might imagine, for example, as a fine, golden human-like parent living in the sky, long white hair and beard looking suspiciously like grandpa, full of love and benevolence towards them and the world? An invisible deity who, moreover, we now know actually exists—to boot!

Sheer indoctrination, of course, you are going to say. And why get their hopes up, when the invisible deity will turn out, eventually, like Father Christmas, and the animals, train engines and clouds that talk, to not exist anyway? Yet they do exist, as we now have to grudgingly admit, and that is why the whole subterfuge has half a chance of working for the average human child, as it did for Abraham back in the day. So, what exactly is the content of this strange, blind, faith in an invisible God, then? Why does it work when it works?

Freud was right to describe it in terms of wish fulfillment. We imagine, yearn for, a God, not in our own image, but in the image of a perfect human being, a perfection of love and goodness and strength, the Über-parent, the Ur-parent of us all, as we have already contemplated. Of course, we initially extrapolate from our actual parents; but, also of course, the perfected image and our faith in it would gradually evaporate as we grow up—as it obviously did for Freud himself—if the God we yearned for didn't actually exist.

Faith, however, is not a sure knowledge of anything—especially when its object is an abstract, universal nothing! As St Paul paradoxically puts it, 'faith is the substance of things hoped for, the evidence of things not seen'.[6] So, it is always in danger of evaporating, regardless of how or whether our parents introduce us to the invisible God who doesn't exist. Freud's father, for example, came from a family of Hasidic Jews and was known for his study of the Torah, the

---

6. Heb 11:1 (KJV).

religious texts of Judaism, including the Hebrew Old Testament; yet his son was a trailblazer of modern, faith-free atheism. Some more profound evidence is needed, surely, therefore, to propel us across the gap from faith in our parents or in anything in our ordinary experience, to faith in the invisible God—to give us a faith that might be enough to compel us to go on a long, dangerous migratory journey at the behest of a voice heard in our imagination; or, for that matter, take the amazing risk—the one that is the central subject of this book—of letting go of our own narrow self-interest and, at least some of the time, even just occasionally, living selflessly for others?

More profound evidence surely; some actual substance, some in-your-face materiality preferably—please! We have glossed over the amazing stories of sin and faith, and God's unfolding plan, post-expulsion from the Garden and prior to the birth of Abraham: such villains/heroes as Cain and Abel, Enoch, Methuselah, Noah and Nimrod. From Abraham onwards we track the exploits of Isaac, Jacob and Esau, Joseph and his brothers, eventually getting to the inimitable Moses, the so-called 'Prince of Egypt' of contemporary fiction, although there is no evidence, in the biblical story or otherwise, that he ever occupied such a royal position. In most cases it is a tale of obedience, or otherwise, to instructions allegedly given to the various protagonists by the invisible God; instructions which often seem reckless, counter-intuitive or even plain dishonest, but invariably work out for the best. This phase, of what is starting to look like a plan by God to achieve an interesting although as yet unclear end, culminates in the Exodus, the escape from Egypt by the Hebrew descendants of Abraham, the final entry into the promised land of Canaan, and, along the way, the so-called Law, the amazing deal or covenant God makes with the people through Moses.

The Law, the Covenant—we will get to that shortly. But again, we cannot help thinking, that is nice for the Hebrews—escaping slavery and finally taking possession of a homeland of their own—but what about the poor Canaanites who made way for them?! 'Now, since European colonisers occupied Australia, much in the way Israel occupied Canaan . . .', a speaker at a forum I attended recently prefaced his remarks with. Yes, European colonization was a systematic mass takeover, by multiple European powers, competing with each other while sometimes being in alliances, over several centuries, of virtually the entire world, made possible by the vastly superior technology and social and military organization of the colonizers, not to say amazing greed and a belief that it was all somehow their God-given right. Yet at the same time, and from the point of view of ordinary European people, sometimes even convicts or exiles, who participated in the colonial project, it was a heroic attempt to escape terrible poverty and social and religious oppression in their countries of origin and make a better life for themselves in the 'New World'.

There is still no solace in this, of course, for the peoples and cultures that were obliterated; but it is, nevertheless, a fallacy, or only a partial truth, to dismiss Abraham's migration to Canaan, then later Moses leading the return of what was by then a much larger group of people to the 'promised land', as a colonising project. Like the poor and oppressed of the present day, Abraham's people were searching for their own 'place in the sun', free from oppressive empires (first the Chaldeans, then the Egyptians), and they were certainly willing to live alongside the Canaanites, make treaties with them, but were forced at different times to undertake military action to take possession of territories they coveted and defend themselves. Yes, like other peoples around them, this included episodes of going too far, of amazing brutality, even mass killings—and then, to cover their tracks, claiming they were just doing as their great God had commanded them! The gall, the iniquity of it: you can read about it all in the Old Testament book of Joshua. But the fact of the matter is that, despite the horrors, the Canaanites were still there, more than a 1000 years later, still a distinct people, living alongside the Jews, likewise under the thumb, at this point, of Imperial Rome.

The Law, the covenant that God unveiled to the Hebrews en route to Canaan—at last, some real substance, some material evidence! There were certainly covenants and laws in the world before this, probably in all cultures, and many, probably, likewise claiming divine warrant; but the test of this one and all those others will be, as we'll see, in the quality of society and polity they lead to. The Mosaic covenant is, firstly, famously, ten commandments written on tablets of stone, brought down from the mountain by Moses, in the wilderness of Sinai; along with an amazing, very elaborate set of rules and regulations governing every aspect of how the people are to live together, under God, when they get there. This is a point in human history: Abraham and his descendants—by this time referred to as the Israelites—God's pet pilot-project, as we've speculated, for teaching humans how to live together in community and society with some chance of not tearing each other to bits. It is also a point in our own history, our own childhood: our parents laying down the law for us, gradually civilizing us, teaching us to consider and respect others, to play by the rules, to show some self-restraint occasionally, to not be so utterly selfish all the time. They may or may not have introduced us to the God who doesn't exist by this point, but either way—for the Israelites as for us—some even stronger medicine, some more profound evidence/substance, will be needed, as we'll see, to finally clinch the deal.

Moses is a remarkable figure, an early archetype, perhaps, of a democratic leader, or, equally, of a modern parent. His awareness of who he is and his calling has a long gestation, and he hides away in a foreign land for many years and even starts a family, seemingly wanting to avoid the great confrontation with Pharaoh that will inevitably come. He is humble, reluctant, self-effacing, even if this initially seems to be driven mainly by fear and feelings of inadequacy. There is certainly no sense throughout his long career that he feels comfortable in the job, and his only role ever seems to be to act as God's agent or prophet; God tells him directly what to do—him and him alone—at virtually every step along the way. But he keeps going bravely and doggedly, despite apparently insuperable odds, and the continued complaining and rebellion of the people.

Yes, the Israelites, like us, grizzle constantly about all the rules and regs; Moses, like our parents, is prone to exasperation and despair, and at one point smashes the original stone tablets to pieces—when he cools down God calmly instructs him to chisel some new ones for them (God) to rewrite the Law on.[7] The covenant Moses presents to the people on God's behalf is a forerunner of modern democratic (and not so democratic) laws and constitutions; just as our parents now act on behalf of those laws and constitutions when they lay down the law for us. But we, and they, continue to bristle and complain, and full-scale rebellion seems ever on the cards. We fear the judgement and punishment of our parents, as they feared the judgement and punishment of God; but in the end, as we know, fear of judgement and punishment are never quite enough to save us from our own self-destructive urges. What they before us, and we now, really need,

---

7. Gen 34.

where the whole covenant thing started, what Abraham truly had, is faith—faith in God's promises, faith in God keeping their side of the bargain.

Faith in an invisible God, speaking to us in our imagination, even when it is mediated by other people, by culture, by nature even. Thus, we have the amazing words that God, 'call[ing] to him from the mountain', gave to Moses to present to Abraham's descendants, the preamble to the covenant God was offering them:

> You yourselves have seen what I did to Egypt, and how I carried you on eagles' wings and brought you to myself. Now if you obey me fully and keep my covenant, then out of all nations you will be my treasured possession. Although the whole earth is mine, you will be for me a kingdom of priests and a holy nation.[8]

'My treasured possession'—my pet pilot-project, we have interpreted it in terms of. A pretty good promise, in anyone's book, but one that seems always to require more courage and, yes, faith, than the ancient Israelites can muster. What follows, then, is the chequered career of the treasured possession/pilot-project that was the Hebrews/Israelites/Jews, from the time of Moses to the final culmination of God's remarkable plan to save the human race, some 1300-1500 years later, now slightly over 2000 years ago.

Our parents make similar assurances to us of a happy and successful adult life to come if we obey the rules—or they do if they want to have half a chance of getting us to do what they say. But what do they have to back up such assurances? Many parents have their own successful lives to point to—that is pretty compelling. Many of us live in countries with real democracy, rule of law, great social institutions and economic prosperity—that is also very compelling. But somehow, no, we don't believe so much in those things anymore. Trust in democracy and civil society is at an all-time low (pollsters are always telling us), parents more than ever worry about the future for their children, with economic disparities, political polarization, climate change and other existential threats, as we rehearsed at the outset of this tale, now hanging menacingly over our heads. Why should we believe our parents, when they don't really believe it themselves?—the great question every new generation now asks.

---

8. Exod 19:4-6.

The assurance back-up our parents traditionally resorted to, in good times or bad, was, of course, the same one Moses resorted to when he wanted to convince the Israelites to accept the covenant he was offering them, namely the great God of Moses' ancestor Abraham, the one who called him (Abraham) out of Ur of the Chaldeans all those years ago. But that God no longer exists for parents to resort to—or at least we don't believe in, have faith or trust in, such a God anymore. Help! Yes, God's apparent disappearance leaves us (parents) now without a leg to stand on when it comes to ministering to our children's most deep-seated fears and anxieties about their own lives and about the world they will grow up into. No wonder everyone is so freaked out—when teenage environmental prophet Greta Thunberg stared at us from our TV screens in 2019 and intoned, 'I want you to feel the fear I feel', it cut us all to the quick to see one so young in such a despairing existential state.

So, yes, some more profound evidence/substance was needed back in the day, and is still always needed now, to finally clinch the deal—to enable us to make the quantum leap across the gap, from limited faith in parents to unlimited faith in an invisible God, from natural human self-centredness to very unnatural selflessness. To make the Law, the Covenant work—so that it is not a burden we always struggle and chafe at, rather a beautiful thing that sets us free to live a better life together, that truly saves us, both individually, and, ultimately, as a species.

What was the next step, then, in the divine plan, the more profound evidence/substance, the final clincher of the deal? Well, what is it in our own lives? We already know the answer: the invisible God of love explicitly presents, turns up, in our lives—the word we're looking for is *incarnates*. The Incarnation: the one human who will, as we speculated at the start of this chapter, save us all, so that through us the whole world will be saved and brought to fruition—or at least have half a chance of not being brought to the edge of extinction. The one human whom it's time I fessed up to you about, therefore, in the next chapter.

Chapter 6
Messiah Complex

The famous Covenant, or Law, of Moses, erstwhile Prince of Egypt, is, as we saw in the last chapter, a blueprint, a plan for a great community, society, nation. Justice, equality, compassion, consideration and respect for others, selflessness, all reign. It is a perfect proto-democracy, no king or queen or absolute ruler to lord it over us, just we the people, free and accountable only to each other, under the endless sky. Or, rather, the ruler is not one among us, ourselves, but the invisible God over all of us, to whom we pledge, each one of us, our allegiance, freely and in faith. Just like in the ideal of modern democracy, God is the *res publica*, the republic, the reification, the embodiment of the collective will of the people.

So, conversely, modern democracies are 'under God' just as much as the original Israelite republic was, even if they make no mention of or explicitly repudiate God—an interesting fact we will look at more closely later. But somehow, the Covenant, the Law was, and is, never enough. Not long after the time of Moses the people of Israel pined for a visible, human king—'Give us a king to lead us . . . We want a king over us!'[1]—and so God the invisible king gave them one, the inconstant and flawed Saul. From there followed the colourful era of the kings of Israel/Judah, the kingdom now split in two, eventually leading to the disasters of the Assyrian, Babylonian then Roman invasions.

Likewise, we, now, eschewing the invisible God and trusting only in ourselves, make heroes out of our democratically elected leaders, then tear them down the next minute when they inevitably, humanly—how dare they?!—make the mistake of not doing exactly

---

1. I Sam 8.

what we want. Modern parents, in turn, look to the wonderful democratic state they may be fortunate enough to live in as back up for their laying down of the law to their children—but, as we have said, their encouragements and admonitions now seem to ring hollow, even if they do find themselves explicitly presenting such assurances. In reality, democratic politics, ancient or modern, always require something stronger at their heart than any individual human, or any humanly conceived formal state structure, can ever provide. Some more profound evidence, some actual substance, some in-your-face materiality preferably.

I wonder if we might have predicted what amazing thing God had up their sleeve next—what more profound evidence/substance, what greater thing than the Law straight from God's own mouth written down on stone tablets—in their plan for our salvation from our self-destructive selfishness? The disillusioned first millennium BCE citizens of the territories of modern-day Israel/Palestine and surrounds, those who claimed their descent back through the sons of Jacob to the original patriarch Abraham, tried to do so. God will send us a *Messiah*, a saviour, an 'anointed one', they opined. Prediction—or maybe just wishful, hopeful thinking? A greater intervention straight from God than the Law, a great high priest, a greater king even than the great David (c 1000BCE), who so loved us, whom we so loved, back in the day?

Greater 'intervention'? The word we will use shortly, as threatened at the end of the last chapter, has a more substantial, material, fleshy ring to it: 'incarnation'. But, yes, the Law could have only come straight from the divine mouth. Perhaps you were thinking that, no, Moses was just an amazingly smart, canny guy, he probably had other (human) collaborators to boot, and he essentially made up the Law himself, later concocting (or others concocting) the lovely story of hearing God calling to him from the mountain, in order to win the people over. When people are gullible enough to believe in the existence of an invisible god you can convince them of just about anything!

You're wrong, however. Sure, humans are very good at making things up off their own bat—we are past masters at it—but not things like the Law. The Law has, at its kernel, an essentially new, non-human idea. Yes, you guessed it (because I have already said it): real faith in an invisible God, faith that is powerful enough to enable you to let go of your own self-interest in favour of the interests of others in your community, faith to trust in each other so that you don't pine for a strong-man human king to lord it over your community and keep it from self-destructing. Faith to live, and love, selflessly together.

Outside intervention, divine intervention in human life, to incarnate, give birth to, put flesh on the bones of, selfless love—yes, that is our familiar notion, the central idea of this book no less. However it happened it must have happened, because we can still today read the actual words it inspired, written 3200 years ago, in modern translations, in the Hebrew Old Testament. Somehow it must have happened, even if the details were not precisely as described in the biblical story—even if the story was written down many years after the fact, by which time the details had changed completely—because no human can ever have come up with the radical idea of it, it's just not natural—faith in an invisible God of love is absolutely, indubitably, essentially, not natural.

Good old Moses; good old God! But it is just a preliminary step along the way, as we have worked out; necessary, but not sufficient, to save us from ourselves. One way or another, we have to grow up, acquire some measure of a faith in life that transcends faith in any specific thing, especially faith in ourselves, so that we take the responsibility ourselves, without looking to any human strong-man or hero to throw our lot in with, without trying to ourselves be that strong-man hero. A faith that empowers us to—some of the time, even just occasionally, or, rather, hopefully, a lot of the time—let go of our self-interest in favour of another—faith that it will ultimately turn out for the best, even if, in the meantime, it turns out badly, even disastrously, for both of us!

We all need a little bit, a non-zero amount of such faith just to get ourselves out of bed each morning, as we've noted. Faith in life, faith in the cosmos, faith in something you obviously can't see but nevertheless sense deep inside yourself—faith, indeed, in the invisible God, the one who doesn't exist but actually does. Your parents loved you, mostly unconditionally, probably; but that is not enough, on its own, to give you such faith. They cannot have failed to present the invisible God to you implicitly (even if it was only the occasional OMG uttered in your presence), since our culture is saturated with the reality of that God anyway—but that's also not enough. They have to go that one step further; they have to, as we have said several times now, present the invisible God to us explicitly: 'Darling, this is God; God, meet darling', etc. They, or someone, or somehow the message has to get through to us—yes, somehow there has to be a breakthrough into our life from the outside, from outside the closed circle of our natural selfish selves.

Invisible God explicitly? An oxymoron, surely? How can you possibly make an invisible God—one who is implicit, hidden, who hides away all the time, who often or even practically always seems to not exist—explicit? Well, how did the invisible God themself do it back in the day? The word is, yes, 'incarnation'. The law, whether written on stone tablets in Moses' time or painstakingly unfolded to us now by our parents, is necessary—it trains and teaches us, it helps us stay alive long enough to give us a half a chance of leading a half decent life—but some stronger medicine/intervention/incarnation is required to enable us to live not by the letter of it but by the spirit, to lead not just a half decent but the best possible life, a great life.

By the spirit not by the letter? It's the simplest thing. To take a humdrum example, why stick to the speed limit when you are driving along the road in your car? The law says do it or you'll be slapped with a speeding fine. So, we stick to the speed limit because we don't want to get a fine? No! We stick to the limit because we care about others, our passengers, other motorists, pedestrians, and so on, whose lives will be impacted for the worse if we speed and something goes wrong. Because we respect the wise traffic controllers who have studied the immediate road and traffic conditions and cautiously and judiciously set the speed limit to maximise safety for all involved. We let go of our own self-interest—sure, I would love to go a bit faster, I am in a hurry and the road's pretty clear anyway—in favour of the personal safety and well-being of others.

That is what the spirit of the law is, as opposed to the letter: caring about, respecting, letting go of our own self-interest in favour of the interests of others. A modicum, as we keep saying, of selflessness, of selfless love. It is the little pedagogical miracle our parents and teachers find themselves tearing their hair out about each day, the impossible task set before them, the most challenging and consequential of all human endeavours. The invisible God in turn was certainly up for the challenge, back in the day. What was required, exactly, indeed, to get human beings across the gap from natural self-centredness to very unnatural selflessness, from a limited natural faith in self or in a stronger self with whom you could ally yourself, to unnatural faith in life itself, in the cosmos, in the invisible God of love?

We are looking back now with the benefit of hindsight, after the fact, of course, but a little while ago we wondered whether we might have predicted what happened before the fact. The people, the descendants of the fabled Abraham who eventually became known as the Jews, put their money, as we noted, on a Messiah, a great king or high priest to one day save them from their enemies. They and many other oppressed peoples around the world, no doubt, back in those days, and even as we still do, as we have noted, in our own little lives today. What was different, distinct about the Jews, however? Well, it might have been in how they saw themselves, as the chosen people of the one invisible God; in the promise they felt they had received, to be a great nation, a blessing to all the nations; in the Law Moses gave to them claiming it had come straight from God's mouth, a blueprint, a pilot-project for a great way of living together in peace and freedom, under God.

Self-chosen, you are probably going to say, a self-appointed divine pilot-project! A collective messiah complex, more likely! And the Law itself, straight from the divine mouth presumably, but necessarily mediated and interpreted through the lens of human ideas, language and culture, was, no doubt, therefore, limited and flawed, at best a rough first draft. But the proof of it, or otherwise, will be in what happens next, in the sort of Messiah who actually comes—or doesn't, as the case may be. And then what happens after that.

The Messiah: a great worldly king/high priest to come? A leader/saviour both temporal and religious? This was the intriguing dual nature of the hoped-for Messiah—ancient culture seeing no distinction between the secular and the religious, a strange way of thinking we are surprised by now in these atheist times. This duality also reflected the fact that the Jews, in a feat of insight so remarkable for its time that it perhaps, as we've suggested, can only be attributable to intervention by the very God we have been talking about, well understood that the predicament they were in, sweating under the yoke of oppressive, corrupt kings of their own, who in turn became mere vassals of even more oppressive empires—Assyrian, Babylonian, Persian, Greek, Roman—was essentially of their own doing. It was the so-called Prophets—famous names like Isaiah, Jeremiah, Ezekiel and Daniel—in the period from the ninth century BCE onwards, who pounded out this message which we can still read in great detail today.

This message: all your troubles are caused by your own faithlessness, your own sin—you have turned away from the Covenant, from the invisible God of love, and you are now reaping the whirlwind. Conversely (as the prophets always then emphasised), if you now turn back to God, if you renew your faith in and obedience to the Covenant, the Law, all will be well: I (the invisible God of love speaking through the mouths of the prophets) will send you the Messiah, the conjoined king/high priest, to save you.

Save you from your sins, your sinful selves—that is the high priest part of it, presumably. But also save you from your temporal enemies—the king part, obviously. This is the double message of the prophets—a Messiah to save us from *both* our sins and our enemies. It is clear, however, that the Law, the Covenant, on its own, did not actually work for the Jews—and orthodox Judaism is still waiting, to this day, for the Messiah to come. The message of the prophets was to repent of your sins, renew your faith in the Covenant—renew living according to its precepts—then get ready for the Messiah. Only when the Messiah arrives will the Covenant be fulfilled, will it work for us.

There is a Catch-22 here, as we have already noted. Keeping to the Covenant, all its rules and regulations, every day, through thick and thin, is hard. Caring for, respecting, loving each other in the way that it essentially requires is hard; and not just hard, but risky, it requires openness, vulnerability, real faith—the sort of faith that, as we have said, is not natural. The sort of faith we can only really get—and here's the catch—when the Messiah comes. It is true, it is paradoxical, we have to receive the Law first, be obedient to it, practise it, live by it, through thick and thin; and only later, after we have done all this, will we be ready to receive the wherewithal, the faith, that is the real blessing, the real fruit of it—both the means and the end of it.

Ah, yes, it is the faith: the Messiah will be the incarnation of faith—faith in the invisible God of love, a 180° reversal of our original sin—the downloading of it into the world, into human life. We (the Jews) are expecting a great king who will save us from our enemies, who will usher in a new kingdom in which justice and goodness and faith reign, but we already have that, implicitly, in seed form in the Law/Covenant, so what is really stopping that new kingdom—that new ideal society under God—from coming into existence is, actually, ourselves, our lack of faith, our (human) inability to selflessly love. We are the enemies we need saving from—not the Romans, or the Assyrians and Babylonians before them—we need saving from ourselves!

The Romans, or the Assyrians and the Babylonians, or any and everyone else on the planet for that matter, are just humans like us, at any rate, and just as much in God's line of sight for saving as are we (Jews). Remember, we were going to be the pilot-project, God's means for blessing the whole world, so it was never just about us. Or so was the line of thinking amongst some Jews, or perhaps growing in the backs of many Jews' minds, when the latest candidate for Jewish Messiah appeared around 1CE, a certain Jesus of Nazareth.

I, a typical European Australian of mixed genetic descent, am part English, part Irish and part, yes, Ashkenazi Jewish—in case you were wondering by what right I dare put thoughts into ancient Jewish minds! The Messiah, along the line of thinking I'm imagining, would therefore very definitely *not* be a worldly king—a strong man, a superhero—but he would, nevertheless, usher in a new kingdom; incarnate, in fact, *The Kingdom*.

The Kingdom—the *Kingdom of God*, the *Kingdom of Heaven*, the *Reign of God*, even the *Republic of Heaven*,[2] lots of names for it—will be the central topic of our next chapter. But what sort of king is this who is not mighty and powerful—not a David, an Alexander, a Caesar—but who nevertheless inaugurates what will become the greatest kingdom of them all, ever? A high priest/king who saves us from our own sinful selves, sets us free to live a life of faith and selfless love, and in so doing plants the seed of an amazing kingdom to come. Sounds great, but, yes, what sort of person, what sort of being, could this Messiah/high priest/king possibly be?

We can see it all in retrospect now because we know, as we saw in Chapter 1, that the faith and selfless love the Messiah was sent to bring into the world is actually now here; and that, as we'll see in the next chapter, the kingdom of it is now growing all around us. But the invisible God was thinking ahead of time: how do I pull it off, how do I get these ornery, uniquely self-conscious creatures over the line to not being so self-centred all the time, before it's too late—before they destroy themselves, before they wipe themselves off the face of the earth?

Obviously, he (the invisible God) must have known what it would take beforehand, before he even created them, *in imago dei*, in the

---

2. David Boulton, *The Trouble with God: Religious Humanism and the Republic of Heaven* (UK: John Hunt, 2002).

image of himself, all those years ago. Ouch!—suddenly I have used a male pronoun for God three times consecutively. But how absurd that I'm even talking about God existing at all! And, for that matter, even if such a God existed, why would that God choose one people alone for a pilot-project of a perfect society, apparently ignoring all others? We have already asked this question. But it gets worse: now the medium through which this God—the one who really exists but is invisible—is supposedly going to deliver the faith and love required to make the pilot-project work, is a single person, a Messiah, who will magically appear in the world in an exclusive place and time, to the exclusion of all other places and times. A king who is not in any way like a normal worldly king but who nevertheless will inaugurate what will become the greatest worldly kingdom of them all. It is absurd, it is implausible, it cannot possibly be true. And even if it is true, it is paternalistic, elitist, exclusionary, more colonial project than pilot-project.

I am referring, perhaps, as I did in the last chapter, to Abraham's descendants colonizing their promised land of Canaan, imposing their God-ordained will on the local inhabitants, negotiating peacefully in some instances, conducting brutal military operations in others. Then I might be referring to the mighty act of colonizing which began with the co-option of the Christian Messiah to the cause of the Roman Empire by Constantine around 313—we will talk some more about that in the next chapter. Beyond that it could be the great European colonising project from the fifteenth century on, the tall-ship invaders carrying with them, among other things (disease, commercial exploitation, slavery, genocide or treaty negotiations at gunpoint) the so-called 'Good News' of the Messiah who had come to them and the kingdom he had apparently inaugurated, imposing it on the poor, unsuspecting, ignorant, innocent ones to whom the Messiah very definitely had not come. And I might be even referring to the re-colonising of Canaan in the twentieth century by the Jewish descendants of Abraham to form the modern, contested state of Israel, at the expense, once again, apparently, of the locals.

Except that the Messiah who had come was not that sort of king, notwithstanding the 'Gospel wrapped in a colonial package' that the good news of him and his kingdom seemed to have become, according to one twenty-first century descendent of Australian Aboriginal people whom I listened to intently at another recent forum, referring to the arrival of Christian missionaries on their shores in the late eighteenth and early nineteenth centuries. And his kingdom was not that sort of kingdom. For starters, this latest candidate for Messiahship, one Jesus, of Nazareth in northern Israel, came to the Jewish people now under the oppressive colonial yoke themselves, of the occupying forces of Imperial Rome under Caesar Augustus. And, even if many Jews were hoping for a Messiah to lead a military uprising against the colonial oppressor, this Jesus certainly had no intention of being that sort of leader.

'Blessed are the meek, for they shall inherit the earth'—the enduring legacy of this man is an amazing collection of one-liners that seem calculated to turn all our old ways of thinking upside down. 'Love your enemies, bless them that curse you', 'if anyone wants to sue you and take your shirt, hand over your coat as well', and so on. Another thing he is recorded as doing a ridiculous amount of is healing people from all sorts of afflictions, physical and mental, including two alleged instances of raising people back to life from the dead. On top of that he seems to have spent much of his time hanging out with all sorts of socially undesirable people—the leprous, the ritually unclean, prostitutes, the possessed, tax collectors, sinners of all stripes. These were not exactly the sorts of things, on any count, you'd expect from the Messiah you'd been hoping for all those years to save you from your enemies and oppressors.

The healings were commonly associated with forgiving people's sins, by the way, and the teachings, through one-liners, parables and, yes, occasional direct language, were always about a way of living that rejected selfishness and embraced selfless love. Ah, the very things we've been talking about all along, the base elements of a greater kingdom, a greater way of living together, to come—that the invisible God who doesn't exist, on one hand, and we parents when we get our act together on the other, have been trying to pummel into our human children all along! Yes, finally, develop a moral conscience, become aware of what a naturally selfish little so-and-so you are, be sorry for all that, then focus on learning to be good, to consider others, to not think the whole world revolves around you all the time. The word Kingdom[3] (I will start using a capital 'K' now) appears in the Gospels as many as 162 times, by some counts, usually straight

---

3. Greek: βασιλεία (basileíā).

out of Jesus' mouth: he did not stint in preaching and proclaiming it, speaking mostly, as usual, in riddles and parables, trying to disrupt our old patterns of thinking and acting, and open us up to a way of living almost entirely new.

But, hang on, this Jesus kept on explicitly pronouncing forgiveness of people's sins, as if he had some magic power to do so. And the healing he seemed to be able to mediate, almost at will, was not merely psychological, but physical, visceral, absolutely tangible—the blind could see, the lame walk, dead people live again, people who had been demon-possessed for a lifetime now free to live normal lives. To compound the fantastical impression he performed other, non-medical miracles, like turning water into wine and walking on water—or so the stories go. Then, on top of all this, as if to explain all this wizardry, he continually told all and sundry that, no, he was no ordinary human, but the 'Son of Man', which was his way, as all the commentators will tell you, of self-identifying as the Messiah.

The disciples and followers of Jesus of Nazareth who eventually wrote down details of his life and explicated his teachings—Matthew, Mark, Luke, John, Paul, Peter, James and possibly others—referred to him as the 'Son of God', or just the 'Son' with a capital 'S'. It is true that 'son of man' (that is, without the capitals) can otherwise refer to just a human being, but either way this Messiah/Son was clearly no ordinary human, rather specially ordained to the task, presumably, by the invisible God; and, yes, why not, in some very real sense, over and above all the rest of us mere mortals, the direct child of that God. So, yes, a real human being, obviously, on one hand; but also, at the same time, somehow, divine—either a god himself in his own right, or perhaps a manifestation (whatever that could possibly mean) of the invisible God themself.

The lines were blurred in those days, at any rate, between humans and gods, so that, for example, around the same time, Caesar Augustus was given the title *divi filius*, 'son of god', and may have badged himself, or been badged by his followers, as an alternative Messiah.[4] The practice was quite common in antiquity, in fact, heroes and rulers often being ascribed divinity, and it has its echoes right down to the present day in the alleged divine right of kings and queens, even in the still extant practice of heads of state doubling as religious leaders,

---

4. See Marcus Borg and John Dominic Crossan, *The Last Week* (San Francisco: Harper One, 2007).

such as the Ayatollahs in Iran or King Charles in Britain. And, yes, obviously, in the prophesied Messiah of the Jews, back in the day, purportedly being both king and high priest.

We may only see a sharp divide between the human and the divine these days because we've decided the divine doesn't even exist—it is pretty hard to be human/divine when the divine is just a figment of your imagination anyway! Thus, Jesus's self-identification as divine 'Son of Man', and his regular references to his 'father in heaven', are now seen as a bit of a brain fade, or even, yes, the original messiah complex. Conversely, however, now that we've come to our senses and realized that the God who doesn't exist actually does, the notion of human/divine circles back into the realm of plausibility.

Is he not referring to a certain divinity that lurks within all of us, perhaps, you might venture. Maybe—and somehow it reaches a certain trigger point with this particular man, his particular circumstances and life experiences, so that we have a unique breakthrough to a new type, a new level, of human life and living—*Humanity 2.0*, perhaps? How ever you think about it, something amazing seemed to occur, some fundamental change in human fortunes, and we are living now in the aftermath. And some sort of divinity breaking through, some explicit intervention from the outside, might be the only possible explanation of such amazingness.

The dual nature of Jesus Christ—'Christ' just meaning Messiah, anointed one—is completely orthodox Christian doctrine, at any rate, ascribed to unrelentingly by the mainstream of the religious movement spawned by the great man, the so-called Christian church (see Chapter 7), to the present day, even if there has been dissenting, 'heretical' voices all along, questioning this frankly paradoxical, contradictory, absurd notion. Some have even tried to imagine some character development for Jesus the man, with a gradually growing awareness during his lifetime of his divinity and his amazing mission on earth— Kazantzakis's agonised tale of a tortured, tormented Jesus in *The Last Temptation of the Christ*, for example[5]—and there are some hints of it in the Gospel stories themselves, for example when a Canaanite woman seems to teach Jesus a thing or two about inclusivity in order to convince him to cast out the demon tormenting her daughter.[6]

---

5. Nikos Kazantzakis, *The Last Temptation of the Christ* [1952], English translation by PA Bien (New York: Simon & Schuster, 1960).
6. Matt 15:21-28.

One way or another, however, looking back in hindsight—and this is something the self-appointed leaders of the church were certainly doing around 325CE in Nicaea (now Turkey), under orders from newly-converted Roman Emperor Constantine, when the paradoxical proposition seems to have first been explicitly formulated—it may be something we just have to take on face value, as a simple fact, I am sorry to say, as the only possible way such a fundamental breakthrough in human affairs could have been made. A solely divine Jesus?—well, that would explain all the magic tricks; but then so what, what else would you expect from a son of a god?! A solely human Jesus?—well, then he was just a liar, or delusional; and all the magic tricks?—well, they surely never actually happened anyway.

I can sense you grinding your teeth over the thought of having to take something so patently absurd on face value. But bear with me. What exactly was it going to take, I want to ask next, this breaking through to a new way of living—this breaking through the impenetrable barrier of sin, selfishness, of living for me, me, me alone; of, yes, living for family, friends, community or nation as well, probably, but all those, as we've said, only as projections of my own egotistical selfish self; certainly not enemies or anyone else beyond that exclusive circle of my personal allegiance, at any rate? What was it going to take for us now to be able to muster the wherewithal, the courage, the gumption, to let go of self and live truly for others, and hang the consequences? Not a crazy, reckless thing, but calculated, intentional, creative—and, yes, as we've said, a small amount of this, a non-zero amount at least, required for all of us, any one of us, to survive, for humanity to survive, for each one of us to get through each day; for the faith and hope of it, even if only unconsciously felt, to enable us to drag ourselves out of bed each morning. What was it going to take? Well, what actually did it take—what actually happened next?

Well, after all the teaching, the healings, the miracles, the forgiveness of sins, the hanging out with losers, you know what happened next. The story of it unfolds gradually through the remainder of the Gospel narratives, and Jesus' followers, disciples were incredulous from the beginning and resisted it to the end, even beyond the end, as we do now. You know it well: the plot by the Pharisees, the betrayal by Judas, the arrest in the garden, the trial, the torture, the crucifixion, brutality unbound. What a story—fact that is stranger and much more amazing than fiction, too amazing to have possibly been made up! Don't go to Jerusalem—what are you thinking?—they will kill you—you are our Messiah, our great king come to save us—start acting like a Messiah—how can you save us if you are dead? Deady-bones dead.

It was the worst thing that could have happened—but it had to happen, apparently. How can we understand it? On one hand there are the clichés: 'the ultimate sacrifice', 'greater love hath no man than he lay down his life for his friends' (actual Jesus words[7]), for example. Yes, fundamentally it was an expression, a modelling of pure selflessness, of selfless love, because (obviously) there is nothing more utterly self-less than letting go of yourself so totally that you give yourself up meekly to be killed. But this is not enough, and on its own makes no sense, because it was a pointless death, a death on trumped up charges; it did not save his friends in any obvious way, his friends did not ask for it, he seemed to be abandoning them. It was a pathetic, miserable death, which only seemed to serve the purposes of the Jewish religious leaders and the Romans. He died and was gone, no use to his friends in the grave, dead as a doornail; gone to oblivion, to a state of being of such utter nothingness that it makes your whole life before it pointless no matter how good a person you have been.

Yes, if you look at the Gospel narratives through rose-coloured glasses, Jesus' whole life was an expression, a modelling of selfless love from start to death. But this was not enough, as I keep saying, and would have made no sense and been truly pointless if that's all it was. So, take the glasses off. Now you are seeing Jesus through the eyes of, let us say, a Nietzsche, or perhaps a Christopher Hitchens or Richard Dawkins. Or perhaps through the Tim Rice imagined mouth of Mary Magdalene, Jesus' famous ex-prostitute disciple: 'He is a man. He is just a man. And I have had so many men before . . .'[8] Let us be frank about it: Jesus the man giving up his life like that was plain dumb, and it basically invalidated all or any of the good stuff he said and did before that, even if you can get past the unlikelihood the Gospel writers were telling his story accurately in the first place.

Let us be frank: if physical death really is the end of it all, then it is not just Jesus' life that is pointless, but all of our lives, all life, mine and yours and even the most mindless microbes that ever crawled

---

7. Jhn 15:13 (KJV).
8. *He's a man*, from *Jesus Christ Superstar*, lyrics by Tim Rice (1970).

out of the primeval slime's lives. Or, to put it another way—and now we're back in Chapter 3—if the universe is purely, solely physical, well we might 'eat, drink and be merry, for tomorrow we die', the mighty doctrine, as we noted back then of YOLO. But it is not (purely and solely physical), and, as we saw, life is a remarkable little phenomenon, which produces a virtuality within organic bodies that goes out into the world to form the collective phenomena of culture, which is where (metaphorically speaking) real purpose and meaning for human life can potentially be found, or at least looked for—and then the God of love whom we have recently discovered must certainly exist, who is the author of all this life in the first place, feeds back into this culture the most amazing grace, the most remarkable instance of which is the very person we are now talking about, the supposed Jewish Messiah back in the day, one Jesus of Nazareth.

Sorry for such an excited mouthful—it's just that it is all starting to make such good sense! We are alive to all this virtuality, we live immersed in it, we are part of it, a constant dynamic flow of it every second of the day; yet we say, no, the universe is only physical, all that stuff that is going on in our heads and in the world around us is just our overactive imaginations, including any idea of God, including any idea that life is more than just physical. We are in an amazing state of false consciousness, so that the very thing that is actually most real to us—our living, breathing, thinking, feeling, imagining self—seems to be counterfeit, an illusion, a dream that dissipates, disappears irrevocably when our physical body can no longer cope with all the excitement and expires for good.

So, yes, as it turned out, the Messiah, who seemed to give up his life for no good reason at all at the tender age of thirty-three, defied all expectations and came rocketing, resurrecting back to life just three days later—by all accounts. Then to compound this death-defying miracle, forty days after that his disciples watched on incredulously as he levitated up into the sky and disappeared altogether, gone back to heaven to be with his God/Father, no longer divine/human, now just divine. What a performance!

Again, how can we understand it? Well, on one hand, again, there is the amazing modelling, demonstration, proof-positive of how to do it—how to absolutely let go of self and live selflessly; to die to self and, so to speak, be born again to a new and greater life of selflessness. A little bit of magic trickery that is, by the way, as we have said repeatedly, essential for all of us, at least a modicum, a non-zero amount of it, to get us through any one of our busy days—to give our entire species, in fact, half a chance of surviving and flourishing into the future. Yes, selflessness is a sort of death and resurrection, a daily out-of-body experience: you imaginatively project your consciousness out of your own body, into the body of the other person, walk a metre or two in their shoes, see the world through their eyes—but not as your own self, rather as an actual other self. You, so to speak, die to your own body then get resurrected in the other person's! It's technically impossible, but it can be done! It's what Jesus modelled, demonstrated, proved, not just by saying and doing all those lovely things while he was alive, but by, in the final moment, rocketing back to life just three days after he seemed to have died. On top of this, the ordinary, occasional little magic trick of selflessness anyone of us might pull off is, therefore, perhaps, a figure of an even greater magic trick we might pull off one day when we follow Jesus' example and rocket back to life ourselves after dying—hopefully!

But no, again, this is still not enough—it is not enough for Jesus just to have modelled, demonstrated, proved that selflessness is possible, even to the extent of miraculously rising from the dead to underline it. Somehow the living power of it has to come into our lives, literally, actually—from the outside, as we always say. Traditionally Jesus' death is understood as, yes, the ultimate sacrifice, but sacrifice in the old, original sense of the word: ritual sacrifice to a god of some possession of yours, which could be an animal or even another human you control, as a substitute or scapegoat for your sins, in order to atone for those sins and thereby mollify and win favour from the god. Thus, Jesus the man, who is also God, ritually sacrifices his own human, physical life to God, in order to win the favour of God for, not himself, but all humanity—the favour, in this case, being formally forever forgiven for all our sinful selfishness and, moreover, somehow set free from the psychological or spiritual power of sinful selfishness over our lives.

I am just relating the traditional formula, the so-called atonement theory[9]: God sacrifices himself to himself in order to atone for our sins and mollify himself. 'I feel better now!', God sings to himself

---

9. For a recent summary of various versions of atonement theory, see Dean Drayton, *Apocalyptic Good News* (Eugene, Oregon: Resource Publications, 2019), 194–6.

after the deed is done. It is an attempt to link the older Jewish tradition of, mostly, animal sacrifice with what was going on with Jesus of Nazareth, and the impression is compounded by Jesus' death apparently occurring on the first day of the traditional festival of Passover, the very day the people made reparation to God for their sins by ritually slaughtering lambs and bringing them to the temple in Jerusalem.[10] But, no, apart from sounding decidedly weird, such explanations ring hollow, because they put the boot on the wrong foot: our problem is not with God, who has nothing but love and good intentions for us, but with our own selfish sinful selves, and the powerful culture of evil around us, the serpent of the Garden story who is always there to tempt us, aid and abet our sinful predilections, help us take our sinning to the next level. Far from being some sort of ultimate, culminating sacrifice, Jesus came to finally put an end to that whole grizzly affair, to sweep away all that old time religion, the endless cults of animal and even human sacrifice, with their futile efforts to please multiple gods who never actually existed.

No, the love-teaching God we are trying to reconstruct in this story does not, cannot, have a side hustle in judgement/reward/punishment; so, the death and apparent resurrection of Jesus must deal directly with whatever real power sin and evil have over our lives, not mollify a cranky deity. Colourful stories are told of Jesus in those three days between death and resurrection going down into hell and setting captives free from the prisons there, fighting and decisively defeating the devil and his evil angels, thereby breaking their stranglehold over the world forever—the compelling image of *Christus Victor*, Christ the Conqueror.[11] Evil still exists and operates in the world, of course, obviously, now 2000 years on, but somehow it has been essentially delimited, neutralized, so that as we channel the spiritual power of true selflessness won by the Christ's victory we can (somehow) overcome its debilitating influences. More than anything the supposed victory is an affirmation, a confirmation of the power of love, greater than human selfishness, greater than any evil the world

---

10. See Shusaku Endo, *A Life of Jesus* [1973], English translation by RA Schuchert (New Jersey: Paulist Press, 1978), Chapter 9.
11. See, for example Gustaf Aulen, *Christus Victor: An Historical Study of the Three Main Types of the Idea of Atonement* [1913], English translation by AG Herbert (London: Macmillan, 1969).

can throw at us: love will ultimately, always, win the day, even if, in the short term, we suffer terribly, or pay with our lives, in its cause.

One way or another, something amazing is claimed to have happened as a result of Jesus' death and subsequent resurrection, which we are now all the beneficiaries of the climax to the whole plan of salvation which started from the expulsion from the Garden. What is available now is, so the story goes, the spiritual power to fuel what is now a full-on universal Kingdom of humanity: the simple ability to love selflessly, to consider and respect others, to live together creatively and harmoniously without wanting to kill each other all the time; and the faith to be obedient to the amazing, evil-defeating, death-defying possibilities of this.

The proof of the pudding will be in the eating, at any rate, which we will consider in the next chapter, the whole story of what happened next up till right now. The plan involved, early on, as we've pointed out, what appeared to be an exclusive choice by God of a particular group of people, the historical Jews, to be a sort of pilot-project, a sort of incarnation in themselves, of the Law/Covenant, right living, a perfect model society. Eventually it narrowed down to one particular Jewish man to be the incarnation of God themself, a sort of pilot-person, the model of a new human, a human now set free from the 'curse' of sin and imbued with the power to truly, selflessly love. Then it narrowed down even further: the man in question was killed, or sacrificed, depending on which way you look at it. But then he rose from the dead, and God is now, apparently, no longer partial, rather the setting free from sin and the power to truly selflessly love is available to all humanity.

Yay! Sounds too good to not be true, as I've said before. It is a little matter of being able to live a greater life now, the best possible life, set free from the selfish grasping that always drags us down; and, it has to also be pointed out, a greater life still beyond physical death. Yes, you heard me, life after death. But before we go on to look at the next part of the story, the unfolding Kingdom that Jesus' death and resurrection ushered in, and the amazing possibilities beyond even that, are we not still troubled by the apparent exclusiveness of this ancient Hebrew God's plan, even if it did eventually become, at least in theory, universal?

Yes, we are. There were gods all over the world back in those days, and there are still the odd one or twenty around even today, many or most of whom don't look particularly like the exclusive one-god of the Hebrews. Were these all counterfeit gods, pretenders to the Hebrew God's throne, really just figments of all these poor, ignorant people's imaginations, false gods fabricated by the people themselves in their own approximate image? Or were they—even the present-day gods of Hinduism, for example, or *Allah*, the one-god of Islam; or the no-god of Buddhism—all actually the same one-God, except only partially or distortedly revealed?

Or, you almost certainly want to also ask, is the Hebrew one-God just one amongst many god-revelations, all equally valid, or, for that matter, all equally invalid? What matters—the only meaningful basis on which we could eventually, decisively hope to answer these questions—is the outcome, the pudding produced by Jesus' apparent death, resurrection and levitation into heaven, which we will start the tasting of in the next chapter. It might help to return to our evolutionary narrative, however, before we do that. In Chapter 4 we contemplated the amazing leap to self-consciousness in the species *homo sapiens*, triggered, it seems possible, not by any natural, material evolutionary process, but by outside intervention of the God who exists—the famous *imago dei*, image of God moment described in the creation story of the Hebrew Old Testament. So now we might consider what we've described as God's Plan of Salvation as itself a series of evolutionary interventions, culminating in the big one, the so-called Incarnation.

Yes, in Jesus, what seems from an evolutionary point of view to be a random mutation occurs, a jump to a new species, *Humanity* or *homo sapiens 2.0*—random it could only seem to the scientific eye, because the actual non-random outside intervention that causes it is by the God who is intentionally invisible. The mutation/incarnation produces a profound psychological or spiritual change, opening up a brand-new trait, giving the organism in question the superpowers of blind faith in an invisible God and the capacity for selfless love.

Sounds implausible, I know, but it seems to have actually happened—the apparent mutation in one human now replicating in other humans, gradually forming a new species—as we'll see in the next chapter. But still, it is exclusive! Why did God wait so long, why choose this one person at this particular place and time, to the exclusion of all others? Why, to take an example close to my home, did it take nearly 1800 years for the Jesus-mutation to reach the shores of the Australian continent, and then only arrive, wrapped, as we noted, in the calamity of British colonization?

We know how evolutionary pressure works: in a general way, across multiple members of a species, varying significantly with localised environmental circumstances. In this case the evolutionary pressure is as we've described it in Chapter 2: the individual psychological necessity of wanting to be loved, which manifests in communities as the pressure to develop positive forms of social interaction and organisation that give the community half a chance of surviving to the next generation—like the pilot-project that was the original Hebrew people we described above. It may be that this unusual little location in the Middle East, a melting pot of civilisations as it was, at that time, was precisely the one location in the whole world where this pressure finally broke through, where the mutation/incarnation in question first burst into human life. Maybe—but that is no solace for all the peoples whose lives and cultures, like the Australian Aborigines, were profoundly disrupted when the alleged mutation/incarnation finally found its way to them. No solace; except that, well, it did (the mutation/incarnation in question) actually, finally, arrive—apparently.

But how—and this is the thing we really want to know more than anything—does it work in our own lives, this mutation/incarnation, this cross/resurrection, this selfless out-of-body magic trick experience, now, 2000 or so years on? If you are a devout Christian believer the answer is straightforward: at a certain point in your life, maybe you are in your teens, you consciously, intentionally accept this self-same Jesus, now apparently operating as a spirit (the "Holy Spirit"), into your lives, and open yourself up to living a new life thereafter of selflessness, serving others and serving God. In most Christian churches there's the formal coming-of-age ritual associated with it, which we mentioned at the start of this chapter, known as confirmation.

Wow, sounds amazing!—but it doesn't always work of course, and maybe you think there are plenty of confirmed Christians out there who are truly bad people! A critical element of the process, however, is utterly telling: repentance. The Greek word this English word translates from the original New Testament writings is μετάνοια, *metanoia*, referring to a complete change of heart, or, even more, a full-on spiritual conversion; but the English word captures the essential first part of the change/conversion in question, namely a profound personal acknowledgement of one's own natural, habitual, sinful selfishness. This is the scary part, the part that puts most people off—none of us want to accept that we are essentially bad. Which is why few people have the courage—or, to the modern way of thinking, the problematically low self-esteem, or just plain stupidity—to do the repentance thing anymore.

It is very unnatural, in fact, for that obvious reason, to be able to acknowledge that you are naturally selfish and sinful. You have to somehow have it impressed upon you, through your participation in the ritual of confirmation, for example, or, as is quite common otherwise, by some terrible disaster occurring in your life which, you are profoundly shocked to realise, is of your own making.[12] Realise?— well, few of us, or perhaps none of us, can even do that off our own bat. It is really only as the invisible God who does exist, intervening from the outside, reveals it to us, through the confirmation ritual or through some other amazing personal revelation, that any of us ever get it through our thick skulls that we are truly, naturally, selfish, bad people.

We have hit a certain nail on the head here. On our own, lost in a natural state of selfish sin, we are powerless to even get to the point of repentance, let alone come out the other side into a new, transformed way of living. Yes, our parents do have to present God to us explicitly, as we speculated earlier; and this means, essentially, presenting Jesus. Or someone has to. But that is still not enough, as I keep saying. No, in the final analysis, Jesus himself, his spirit, has to come to us, has to do the revealing, the impressing upon, himself—our own private, personal, individual incarnation, you might say. All we can do is, somehow, be open to it. Or maybe even that's not enough? Or too much? We might want and want and want it to happen (Jesus coming to us), but maybe the act of wanting is the very thing that gets in the way?!

So, yes, it is the easiest thing in the world for someone to go through the ritual of confirmation, or some other experience that leads to repentance, but not actually be changed deep down, then continue muddling on through life, as we all do, still prey to our own selfish grasping and its self-harming consequences, still an easy target

---

12. In modern psychology *metanoia* refers to 'the process of experiencing a psychotic 'breakdown' and subsequent, positive psychological re-building or 'healing" (see the Wikipedia article)—a definition which very nicely captures the New Testament meaning.

for the latest predatory cultural evil that comes along. Conversely—you have probably been wanting to say this all along—it is perfectly possible for people to be good, to act selflessly, to be a decent person, without any interest in or contact with Christianity at all—no explicit God presentation, no Jesus really necessary, apparently.

There is no doubt this is true—in fact the whole argument of this book hangs on it! On one hand we can only assume that the invisible God has been busy working everywhere, at all times, with all peoples, focussing on this one central thing, teaching us how to love, how to live together in creative harmony without tearing each other to bits. On the other hand, and zeroing in on the present day, right now in the twenty-first century, human culture must be, presumably, positively saturated with whatever spiritual power of selflessness came into the world through the figure of Jesus of Nazareth back in the day—the mutation has replicated, multiplied, spread widely, you might say. As we will see in the next chapter, one of its fundamental expressions is in amazing democratic culture and institutions that now flourish in many parts of the world. So, no wonder any child born today will develop some facility with selflessness—considering and respecting others, playing nicely, obeying laws, being a good citizen, caring for the poor and vulnerable, participating in democratic culture generally—regardless of, in most cases, having never been explicitly introduced to God/Jesus; except perhaps for, as we've said, over-hearing their parents' casual *OMGs* and *Jesus #$@&%** from time to time.

Yes, the power of it has certainly been in the world, probably from the beginning. But, no, there is still something utterly necessary about it becoming explicit—about the explicit incarnation of God historically, at a certain place and time 2000 years ago, and the explicit incarnation in each of our lives now. Otherwise, we will always, inevitably, sooner or later, revert to our selfish, self-destructive natural selves. Perhaps it is the profound danger of this that we sense in the present day, with our fears for the future, our fascination with dystopian fiction, our visions of impending environmental doom—in these days when the God who claimed to have saved us from self-destruction and set us on a new path seems to no longer exist. Perhaps . . . but the God in question does still exist, as you and I have recently discovered. So let us now, in the remaining chapters of this book, turn our attention to the great hope for the future this unexpected, rather shocking discovery brings: the hope, as we've noted, and as the erstwhile Messiah who gave his name to this chapter couldn't stop talking about back in the day, of an amazing Kingdom to come. A coming Kingdom? For a Kingdom surely you need a pilot-project to get it started? Well, as we've seen, the God who still exists was into pilot-projects right from early on: first it was the ancient Israelites under the old covenant of Moses, then it was the one-man pilot-project that was Jesus of Nazareth, what will it be now?

Chapter 7
The Church and the Counterfeit Gospel

A Kingdom coming, a pilot-project for it. The Kingdom in question, as we saw in the last chapter, is no mystical otherworldly paradise but a very concrete potential future state of human relationships in this world, based on selfless cooperation—which, by the way, as we've seen, we have no choice but to evolve towards if we want to avoid the terrifying opposite, namely hell on earth and probable extinction. A state of human relationships based on selfless cooperation, on individuals letting go of their own self-interest in favour of the interest of the group: sounds suspiciously like the ideal of democracy—and it is!

A pilot-project for it: this was the purpose of God's so-called 'plan of salvation', culminating in the 'incarnation', some 2000 years ago, of the amazing Jesus of Nazareth, which we tracked in the previous three chapters of this book—the God whom we had spent the first three chapters establishing the likely, real existence of. It's referred to as a salvation plan because in order to develop the capacity for selfless cooperation we have to be saved from the opposite: our natural-born, individual propensity for non-cooperation, for selfishly pleasing ourselves all the time, hang everyone else. And this salvation is far from being just an individual thing, as we saw: we are collective creatures, and our individual selfishness goes outwards into the virtual, cultural space around us, forming the many structures of evil that influence our individual lives and ever threaten our survival as a species. This very real, concrete threat generates an evolutionary pressure which has, among other things, as we saw in Chapter 2, spawned religions, traditional and modern, all of which, in one way or another, seek to facilitate our transition from natural selfishness to unnatural selflessness. But no effort of our own by itself can possibly pull off such a miracle, so, at the same time, as we eventually realised, the God whom we long thought didn't exist was busily, invisibly, working away in the background, all along, to provide us with the ways and means to develop the capacity for selflessness. All religions? Well, we tracked God's actions through one particular religious tradition, the Judaeo-Christian: hence Jesus of Nazareth.

A selfless love teaching God with a salvation plan: the plan—the Judaeo-Christian version of it, at any rate—involved, first, a pilot-project people, the ancient Hebrews or Israelites, descendants of the patriarch Abraham; then a one-man pilot-project, Jesus himself. After Jesus' departure at the tender age of just thirty-three—he simply ascended into the sky and disappeared for good—the pilot-project passed over to the great man-god's original band of disciples, numbering a dozen or more, who formed the nucleus of what has come to be known as the Christian church, the now global mega-institution we are all familiar with. So, the Kingdom coming and the pilot-project for it: let us now start tracking the story of them both as Jesus' followers set out on this great mission he had prepared them for.

The word *church* first appears in the biblical narrative straight from the mouth of Jesus himself:

> And I tell you that you are Peter, and on this rock I will build my Church, and the gates of Hades will not overcome it.[1]

Peter is the de facto leader of the disciples, Jesus' closest followers, and there may be some play on words going on here, because 'Peter' in Greek pretty much means rock.[2] The context is compelling: Jesus makes this statement immediately before he begins unveiling to the disciples the discomfiting news that he will very shortly die. The church is what the disciples will do—the amazing movement they will found—after he is gone.

The Greek word of the original text translated in English as *church* is ἐκκλησία (*ekklesia*), meaning, roughly, 'called out ones'. So, a community of people called out from the surrounding religion and culture, to be distinct from it—to be different and in some way special—but not separate. To be, yes, specifically, a pilot project for the Kingdom Jesus spent so much time preaching about, a great

---

1. Matt 16:18 (NIV).
2. In Greek the name 'Petros' is, literally, 'detached stone', and 'rock' is 'petra'.

way of living together, based on the very unnatural selflessness that now becomes truly possible through his death and resurrection. Not a hermit kingdom, rejecting the world, doing its own thing, rather one which continually reaches out to convert the society and culture around to this new way of life.

What an amazing idea—if that is what it really was! The 'called out' aspect of the Christian Church is distinctive, critical. It follows the biblical pattern: in Chapter 5 we saw how the patriarch Abraham was called out from the Chaldean country and culture of his birth, his Jewish descendants later becoming the original divine pilot project. Jesus' followers are now in turn being called out from that first pilot to form a new project community, one which is no longer focussed exclusively on the Jewish people but open to all-comers.

Called out to be a pilot project, for all humanity, a seed community that will grow, reproduce and eventually transform the whole world. No other religious tradition seems to give birth to such a notion, such a phenomenon. A religious community set up with the purpose of not just being itself, taking care of its own people, but of gradually converting, transforming the society and culture around. An inclusive, open, organic, growing social structure rather than one which is closed, static, exclusive. Synagogues, mosques, ashrams, temples and the like are, for the most part, conservative institutions, which either support the dominant social and political structures of the societies in which they are embedded—typically hierarchical, autocratic, non-democratic—or at least present no critique of them.

At that point, however, Christianity was not yet a religious tradition, even if it soon became one, so the original communities were not really religious. Quite the contrary: organised, institutional religious culture was the very thing the communities were called out from, the mainstream Judaic and other cultures of the day around them, the old religious beliefs and practices, the false gods and God of judgement and punishment who oppressed them spiritually far more than their Roman overlords oppressed them in the flesh. Christianity, at the outset, was essentially anti-religion, post-religion, religionless, a movement which reached out beyond itself to the society around, beyond all culture and religion to the invisible God of love above.

That is the theory, at any rate: that the church, the movement founded by Jesus' followers, is, uniquely, as I am claiming it to be, post-religion, an agent of profound personal, social, cultural transformation. But by the time we get to the Constantinian settlement in the early fourth century CE you would have thought the opposite! The church is now allied with the Roman imperial state and has taken on a socially conservative hierarchical structure with a supreme leader, the Bishop or Pope of Rome, the first of whom was, allegedly, the self-same Peter we met a little while ago, the rock foundation of what is now a mighty socio-cultural institution. The emperor is now the church's enforcer-in-chief: of doctrine, practice, order and unity, proper worship of the invisible God who doesn't exist. Or is it the other way round: the emperor converts the church, adopts it as one of his key enforcers, maintains and extends his power through its agency?

Nothing in what Jesus says in the Gospels, or in the writings of the other New Testament authors, anticipates this outcome—unless you want to retrofit it in after the fact, as church leaders later essentially did! The earliest Christian communities, documented in the New Testament Book of Acts, written around 70–90 CE, bore little resemblance to what the church later became. These communities were the first fruits of Jesus' radical call to selfless living in community. He had urged his followers to be 'the light of the world'[3]—a pilot-project for all humanity, as we have described it—and here is a neat firsthand description of how one of these communities operated:

> They devoted themselves to the apostles' teaching and to fellowship, to the breaking of bread and to prayer. Everyone was filled with awe at the many wonders and signs performed by the apostles. All the believers were together and had everything in common. They sold property and possessions to give to anyone who had need. Every day they continued to meet together in the temple courts. They broke bread in their homes and ate together with glad and sincere hearts, praising God and enjoying the favour of all the people. And the Lord added to their number daily those who were being saved.[4]

Sounds a bit like a modern commune, a primitive form of socialist utopia—but actually it is not. You might think, for example, that the little phrase 'praising God' is an optional extra that could easily be

---

3. Matt 5:14.
4. Acts 2:42–47.

left out without changing the nature of the community; but in fact, as we've realized, this God is actually real, and, moreover, is the one who inspired the founding of the community, who rendered this group of human beings even capable of living together in such a selfless and devoted way in the first place. The worship of—the intentional listening to, the seeking of comfort and inspiration from—the God who really does exist, is the core activity of the community, the very thing, the only thing, that makes it work.

There's a reason why communes, socialist utopias don't work; why, over time, they typically disintegrate or die out because of internal conflict or plain lack of motivation: there's simply no God to worship, no really existing being outside of our human selves to seek inspiration from—if only because socialism in its most ideological forms explicitly repudiates any such God. All that's left to inspire the comrades is some notion of universal siblinghood, a purely human construction which boils down ultimately to nothing more than a fixed, abstract ideal of material equality. You end up worshipping, not a real living, loving being, but the very material property and possessions you are trying to set yourself free from, exchanging, in the process, one tyranny—material inequality and poverty—for another—inflexible, authoritarian enforcement of material equality.

'All the believers . . . had everything in common. They sold property and possessions to give to anyone who had need.' This certainly sounds like socialism, but before it is socialism it is, in fact, democracy. The believers are acting out of the freedom that comes from letting go of self and living for others, not a purely intellectual commitment to an abstract ideal, which, in the end, only serves to disguise the fact that we are actually really only interested in living for ourselves. Freedom to share our lives together, mutual support, acceptance of diversity; 'from each according to his ability, to each according to his needs'—a neat phrase, attributed to Karl Marx,[5] but which some commentators trace to this follow up passage in the book of Acts:

> All the believers were one in heart and mind. No one claimed that any of their possessions was their own, but they shared everything they had . . . And God's grace was so powerfully at work in them all that there were no needy persons among

---
5. Karl Marx, *Critique of the Gotha Programme*, 1875.

them. For from time to time those who owned land or houses sold them, brought the money from the sales and put it at the apostles' feet, and it was distributed to anyone who had need.[6]

We'll hear more of Marx in the next chapter, but this is also the point of departure, as it turns out, from original Greek forms of democracy. The freedom that is the essential element of the early Christian communities is a letting go of power or control over your own life, not a hanging on to it but sharing it around amongst a limited group. It is not, to be specific, the sharing of control over the means of production (as in the case of socialism) or sharing of political control (in the case of Greek democracy). The word *democracy* itself betrays the real motivation of the earliest democracies, in contrast to what was driving the original Christians: δῆμος-κράτος (*demos-kratos*), *people-power*, as opposed to autocracy or oligarchy—the people seize power from the traditional autocrat or oligarchs and share it amongst themselves—no letting go of power intended or even thought of!

The 'people'? Well, not quite. In the Athenian city-state circa 600 BCE, for example, only citizens, numbering less than 30% of the adult population, were allowed to participate in the political system; women, slaves, foreigners, the majority of the population, were excluded, and therefore effectively subject to the same tyranny that the 'people' had historically experienced under autocrats and oligarchs. Athenian democracy was certainly an amazing innovation, going in the right direction—of a more just and equitable society—but it lacked a critical something, which ensured it was only a relatively short-lived experiment, doomed to be swamped, as was the later Roman republic, by the tide of Greek and Roman heroes and emperors to come.

The critical something: letting go of power or control over your own life, a sharing not of power, but of powerlessness. Where does the power go, in this new conception of people-power the early Christian communities modelled? To the invisible God of love over all, in obedience to whom the believers serve each other selflessly and reach out to others in the world beyond, to the poor, the sick, the rejected especially, as the church typically does to this day, to anyone who is inspired to join in the work and live the great life the community has to offer. 'And the Lord added to their number daily those who were being saved'—it worked pretty well in other words!

---

6. Acts 4:32–35 (NIV).

There is a world of difference, in fact, between a bunch of mates bandying together to overthrow a tyrannical autocrat, then sharing the power amongst themselves to the exclusion of the majority, and an inclusive community which reaches out and opens up to all-comers, regardless of power, status, material wealth. The original ideal that inspired the early Christian communities was, as it turned out, the beginning of everything we now identify with the modern welfare state, from hospitals and health care to unemployment relief and care for refugees and migrants. And, yes, democracy with universal suffrage and potentially 100% participation in the political system, unrestricted by social circumstance, gender or religion.

That is the theory, at least—as we have already noted—and it all sounds straightforward, fabulous. But, yes, it didn't quite go according to plan, or at least to what we might have thought the plan would be. We've already noted that by the fourth century CE the church was looking more like a projection of Roman Imperial power than a prototypical democracy; now institutionalised and with an elaborate hierarchical structure, it had already become, to all intents and purposes, the very thing it set out not to be, not a pilot project for the coming Kingdom but a little kingdom unto itself! But let's backtrack even further, to certain features of the teachings of Jesus and the writings of the early church's great apostle, St Paul.

'Render unto Caesar the things that are Caesar's,' so the famous expression goes, 'and unto God the things that are God's.'[7] The words are attributed to Jesus by three out of the four Gospel writers, and the context is the great man cleverly wriggling out of a trap set by his constant opponents, the Jewish religious leaders of the day, the Scribes and Pharisees. His constant opponents: not the imperial Roman authorities, the evil occupiers and colonisers of Palestine and Judea of the day, with whom he seems mostly on good terms— there is the well-known story of Jesus healing a centurion's servant on account of his (the centurion's) faith[8]—even to the point of ultimately submitting passively to their torture and execution.

'My kingdom is not of this world', he says at another point.[9] You have the clear impression that the fabled Kingdom Jesus constantly

---

7. Mk 12:17 (KJV).
8. See, for example, Matt 8:5–13.
9. Jhn 18:36 (NIV).

talks about, that the church becomes the pilot-project for, is, as he goes on to say, 'from another place'. It is not, in other words, a coming future objective state of human relationships in this world, as we've described it, but a kingdom beyond this world, a heavenly kingdom perhaps, one we only get to enter into after we die and, even then, only if we are fortunate enough to have been 'saved'. Clear impression? Except that Jesus is famously ambiguous and speaks about the Kingdom mostly in parables, and when you put everything he says together and note, as we did in the last chapter, that the core content of his teaching as a whole is selflessness in human relationships right here and now, you get the clear impression that his Kingdom *is* of this world. Go figure!

It is the commonest and most fatal of misapprehensions—I would say—that the Kingdom Jesus was talking about is not this world but another one. A second, related misapprehension has it that the Kingdom is purely an internal psychological or spiritual state.[10] Either way, the Christian's clear task is, therefore, to not in any way subvert the political status quo, rather to comply with it honestly and to the best of your ability. As for Paul, his view, expressed on multiple occasions in his various letters to the early Christian communities, is that the Kingdom will come only in the unforeseeable future, when Jesus returns,[11] and that our task now as believers is to endure whatever suffering comes our way, remain steadfast to the cause and await the great day. Yes, as we will explore in detail in Chapter 9, it appears that Jesus had promised his disciples that he would return to earth again one day—the so-called 'Second Coming'—and this would in some sense bring the Kingdom to fruition. There's a sense of its imminence in Jesus' statements on the subject, in fact, as we'll see, and certainly the disciples and many of the early Christians, including Paul, believed Jesus might return any moment, in their own lifetime probably.

Unforeseeable but imminent! If the Second Coming is tomorrow, there is not much time today for a pilot-project, we would be better off just concentrating on getting our own souls, our own communities

---

10. Based usually on the King James rendition of Lk 17:21: '. . . neither shall they say, Lo here! or, lo there! for, behold, the kingdom of God is within you.' Other translations have 'among' or 'in the midst of', which make it clear that an internal state is probably not intended.
11. See, for example 1 Thess 2:12, 2 Thess 1:5, 2 Tim 2:12 and 4:1.

together. So, with Paul we have this interesting ambiguity, socially and politically both progressive and conservative. The early communities under his tutelage were radically inclusive for the time, for almost any time: no distinctions of race, class or gender; male and female, Jew and Gentile, slave or Roman citizen, all equal before God—at least in theory. But at the same time Paul, for example, accepted slavery, and was happy to make good use of his Roman citizenship when it suited him, seeking refuge and protection from the Roman authorities when the local religious leaders were on his tail, even if, as the story goes, he was eventually executed in Rome during a notorious persecution.

We will attempt to fathom this strange notion of a second coming in detail later, as I said; but, as it turned out, Jesus didn't come back tomorrow! The damage was done, however, and since that day the mainstream view of Christians and the church is that the Kingdom is *not* here and now, *not* a gradual transformation of this present world, for which the church is a pilot-project, as I have persistently asserted. Not an unforeseeable future state of this present world attendant on the return of Jesus even, for in our fears and pain and suffering of the present moment we have needed something much closer to give us comfort and hope, the hope of an instant release from our pain and suffering at the moment of our own individual death no less, an entry into a heavenly realm, a paradise, a blessed afterlife.

Yes, the view that Jesus will return tomorrow to solve all our problems has persisted intermittently right to the present day, with crazy doomsday cults still popping up to shock us every now and again; but the mainstream, popular view has become one of a happy afterlife now in another world altogether, with belief in a literal second coming of Jesus fading into an unknowable and therefore effectively irrelevant future. The interesting irony is that belief in an immediate otherworldly afterlife was common to the many so-called 'pagan' religions around the place at the time that Christianity purported to refute and replace—the Egyptian, Greek and Roman cults are obvious examples—whereas it seems to have been of no great concern in pre-Christian Judaism, there not being a single unambiguous mention of a happy afterlife in the Hebrew Old Testament.

Modern liberal Christianity, which we'll get to in the next chapter, reacting against mainstream popular belief, has vanquished not just the Second Coming but the afterlife Kingdom itself also; so that, either way, there is now not much left of a Kingdom in this present world at all. It is an amazing departure from the 'good news' of the Kingdom, the Gospel, Jesus was announcing—an inversion almost. We can well understand how it happened. The early Christians were frequently under the pump, fearing for their lives, and they had just seen their erstwhile leader pursued and trapped by the religious authorities, by their own people, then brutally, almost casually, tortured and murdered by the imperial occupiers. So, yes, out of fear, out of the pain and suffering we experience now, out of the apparent enormity of the task ahead of us, we give up hope in this current world and look to a life beyond death for our succour. Or we give up even that, no longer capable of the feat of imagination, or fantasy, required, so that the present world as we see and understand it is going nowhere in particular or, worse still, more likely, going down the gurgler fast, no Kingdom in sight either way.

Out of fear. Or, alternatively, out of pride, out of over-confidence in our own abilities, the very thing that, as we saw, got us into trouble in the first place—'we can do better ourselves, we don't need you [God]; and, come to think of it, you don't exist anyway'—so that we create the Kingdom, the perfect world ourselves, with our science, technology and industry, our great learning, our civilization, the humanist dream, no God required, we are God. But then things go wrong, as they seem to have done most recently with our present polycrisis, and we bounce back the other way, to fear and despair. It is, yes, an amazing departure, an almost complete inversion; somehow out of fear or pride we manage to create this inverted, counterfeit version of Jesus' Gospel, something that looks superficially like the real thing but is actually, as I've said, a fatal misapprehension of it.

A counterfeit Gospel—fake good news, you might say! On the back of it the church makes itself a substitute for the real Kingdom, a little kingdom of its own—and this was certainly the case by at least the fourth century CE, as we have noted several times now. Not that life beyond the grave, a mini resurrection of our own, is, as we noted in Chapter 6 and will contemplate again in Chapter 9, beyond the realms of possibility, it is just that when our primary focus is not on this life, this world now, we're in immediate danger of going astray. Suddenly our attention and concern shift to the next life, to the question of how we can ensure we make the cut. The old fears flare up: maybe I will always be alone, imprisoned in my own self-conscious self, alienated from all other selves, from the cosmos itself, maybe not even death would release me from my prison, maybe death would only serve to render my imprisonment eternal? The old, existential human fears that, as we saw in Chapter 4, have always been with us: the panic attack, the little child's tantrum, the despair, I will never be good enough, everybody hates me, people will never accept me, not even God will accept me.

We are back, by an amazing irony, where we were before the incarnation, in fact, with the God we're trying to please whom we can never please—if only because they don't exist! This is the place where, for example, the great Luther found himself immediately before his breakthrough, or break back, to the original, true Gospel: how can we ever be sure, how can we ever know, that our efforts, our works of being good, being obedient, truly and selflessly loving God, will be enough, will enable us to make the cut? Surely this is a fearsome, judgemental God, our salvation always uncertain, always seeming to hang in the balance: heaven might be something to look forward to, but if I miss out, hell doesn't bear thinking about!

Efforts, works, obedience, trying hard to love a God whom we're actually terrified of and whom, for that very reason, we secretly resent: yes, this is where we were before the incarnation. We're making sacrifices, burnt offerings, propitiating, begging the gods to be nice to us, performing elaborate rituals to show them what good people we are. We are the little child seeking the approval of parent or teacher, trying hard to be good despite it seeming so petty and pointless, before it begins to dawn on us that it is our motivation that matters. That what wins the gods and our parents' approval is the heart we're showing and that, at any rate, the genuine selflessness we are now practising and are beginning to do so almost naturally— consideration of others, care, respect, thoughtfulness, humbleness even, living together harmoniously in community—makes us feel great, ourselves, anyway.

We've been here before—obviously! This counterfeit Gospel, that we so easily and naturally slide back into, has us desperately trying to work our way to heaven—has us, full of pride and self-belief, imagining we can actually do so—trying to save ourselves, so to speak, by our own good works. 'Salvation by works', in fact: that is how the great reformers, especially Luther, badged it, some 1500 years on from the Jesus-incarnation—an essentially pre-incarnation notion that had by then long since become the standard belief and practice of the now millions of folk who were trying, in many cases very earnestly, to follow Jesus' example.

Yes, counterfeit, pre-incarnation. But why in the world did anyone believe it? Well, because of what the church had become on the back of it: a little kingdom unto itself, a worldly, institutionalized, exclusive salvation gatekeeper. The church held the 'keys of the Kingdom': it dispensed entry to the afterlife through its many sacraments, through (up to the time of the Reformation) the infamous sale of indulgences and other cash-generating products, most of all through enforcing the obedience of the faithful to its many rules and regulations. Enforcing? Only by allying itself with worldly power, by becoming worldly power itself, could it have hoped to do so—and it did.

A kingdom unto itself: we see this clearly already by the time of St Augustine, Bishop of Hippo in North Africa 395–430 CE, writer of many books and preacher of a thousand sermons. Now there are not one but two kingdoms, or rather cities, developing in parallel, geographically intermingled and inseparable until the ultimate Second Coming of Christ. The 'City of God', whose citizens are all those who truly reject sin and cling to God, and the worldly, earthly city—the 'city of Satan' as Augustine sometimes referred to it—consisting of all people who continue to embrace sin, who choose to themselves be gods.[12] We can never know which of the two cities we are in, Augustine surprisingly claims, so that when Jesus' returns and God institutes his final judgement many in the church will unhappily discover they in fact haven't made the cut; likewise, many now outside the church, surprise, surprise, actually will make the cut.

As is well known, Augustine's central concern was to defend his new found Christian faith—he converted at age thirty-two, in 386 CE[13]—against accusations that Rome's still only very recent rejection of the old pagan gods in favour of the new cult of Christianity was the cause of its now being in dire straits, with barbarian hordes at every doorstep—hence the full title of his most famous work, *Concerning the City of God, against the pagans*. But to do so he had to come up with a formula which separated the church out from all other, worldly cities, as a city in itself, so that worldly cities, kingdoms and empires might come and go, but God's City, Kingdom or Empire, being of an essentially distinct nature, can and will last forever.

---

12. Saint Augustine, *Concerning the City of God, against the pagans* [413–427CE], English translation by Henry Bettinson (London: Penguin, 1972).
13. Saint Augustine, *Confessions* [397-8CE], English translation by RS Pine-Coffin (London: Penguin, 1961), Book VIII Chapter 12.

A millennium later, Luther—a devout Augustinian monk in a previous life—propounded his famous 'doctrine of the two kingdoms',[14] and, despite blowing the whistle very loudly and consequentially on just how far the Roman Church had diverged by that time from the true Gospel, there was no question in his mind that church and state were not distinct entities, even if he was still adamant that the state had not just the right but the responsibility to impose a particular type of church, Protestant preferably, on all its subjects. The consequence was that, in Luther's view of the world, earthly authority was free still to be as autocratic and authoritarian as it wanted to be, and even if it oppressed its people, the Christian's job was not to oppose it, but to acquiesce patiently, even long-sufferingly, to its demands.

Religious toleration and full separation between church and state were still a long-time coming in Christendom, but the die had been cast already, long before, before Luther, before Augustine, Constantine, before Jesus even. It was a die the God who exists sent Jesus to uncast, as we noted in the last chapter, hence the amazing irony of an almost immediate reversion to type by the church Jesus' followers founded. Augustine's heavenly city, as he developed the idea of it, was a city of the *soul*, in contrast to the earthly city of the *body*. Soul-city citizens were still subject to the laws of the other city and reliant on it for material needs, but they remained ever, essentially, outsiders, alien sojourners in it, living good, responsible lives in the meantime, patiently awaiting the day of final liberation.[15] It's a dualistic conception which—more amazing irony—surely comes straight from the doctrines of the thoroughly gnostic Manichaeism that Augustine converted from and went to such great lengths to refute in his most famous book.

'Superstitious, soul-destroying fallacies', Augustine described his former beliefs as, post-conversion.[16] Mani (216–274 CE) was a famous Persian mystic, founder of a religion which has a small number of adherents still to this day, surprisingly in China.[17] But gnostic belief in general has its roots deep in human prehistory, exerting an important influence on virtually all religious belief and practice, popping its head

---

14. See, for example, *Von Weltlicher Obrigkeit* (On worldly authority) 1523.
15. Saint Augustine, *City of God*, Book XVIII, Chapter 1
16. Saint Augustine, *Confessions*, Book VIII Chapter 12.
17. Chinese Manichaeism, also known as *Monijiao* or *Mingjiao*.

up all over the place including, as I am suggesting, in the thinking of Augustine the avowed anti-Manichaean and, yes, in the counterfeit Gospel Luther only partially exposed. It is pretty much as Augustine described: we are souls in a sort of exile in a physical body, in a fallen material world, the temporal setting of a great cosmic battle between good and evil, and all we can do is place ourselves on the side of the good and strive towards some sort of liberation from this evil body and evil world. For Augustine, Christianity 'offers a universal way for the liberation of the soul'[18]: it is a matter of repenting of your sins then submitting yourself to the authority and direction of the church, living a life of good works thereafter, keeping your fingers crossed it will turn out in the end you really are a citizen of the City/Kingdom of God. For Gnostics, by contrast, it's not repentance that gets you over the line but secret, esoteric knowledge of God, which you can glean by yourself, without a gatekeeping church, although invariably there's some sort of appropriate religious expert—a priest, shaman, guru or seer—to guide you on the way and whom you'd do well not to ignore.

There are still adherents of Gnosticism today, the Mandaeans in Iraq and Iran and diaspora communities, but there's a gnostic inside all of us anyway, I would hazard, a fear or proud hope that I, myself, personally might be a chosen one who might be able to secretively escape this terrible, ugly world, in spirit if not in body. It is an appealing belief, makes a lot of sense. As a child I found no succour, no relief in moments of despair or depression, in prayer to a God who seemed to almost certainly not exist, or in participation in the formalities of the Catholic church I was raised in. So, I sought it instead in fantasy, finding myself one day aged about thirteen alone in my backyard reciting the incantation specified, in one of CS Lewis's wonderful children's books, that would enable you to enter the fabled land of Narnia. It did not work, of course, but I have harboured feint gnostic hopes ever since! And the Narnia books, as well as Lewis's *Cosmic Trilogy*: is not it remarkable to realise just how gnostic they are, Lewis ever the great Christian apologist—but more on the great cosmic battle between good and evil a bit later in our story.

Repent or don't repent: it doesn't matter either way if you have got the wrong idea of what you are repenting from. All these things are confused and tangled up in the pre-incarnation beliefs that evolved,

---

18. Saint Augustine, *City of God*, Book X, Chapter 32.

as I have suggested, into a counterfeit version of the Gospel the church still doesn't seem to have broken free of. We are back near the start of Chapter 4 in fact: the sin we need saving from is not individual acts of disobedience to some sort of law or moral code, but our amazing propensity for doing such things that stems from our natural-born self-centredness. So it is not so much repentance and forgiveness for individual acts of disobedience that we need—there would be no end of it if that was all there was to it, no guarantee that we might not lapse into one final bout of yet to be forgiven sin shortly before we die, and in doing so blow our chances of making it to the happy afterlife— as Augustine and later Luther, as we saw, agonized about. Rather it is *metanoia*—the Greek word in the New Testament translated into English as 'repentance' (we're in Chapter 6 now)—that we need, a complete change of mind, a radical transformation of mindset from one of natural selfishness to one of very unnatural selflessness.

Yes, don't bother repenting if all you see it as is getting forgiven for your latest batch of sins—stay a natural gnostic instead and hope for the best! One thing leads to another, however: when you mistake sin for individual acts of disobedience you get tangled up in the various versions of the 'atonement theory' we contemplated in Chapter 6, seeing Jesus' death on the Cross as a sacrifice to mollify a grumpy deity whom we—all humanity—have had the temerity to disobey all these millions of times. The deity we're imagining—the God who doesn't exist—is not just grumpy but plain stupid: for starters they are basically, as we noted back then, sacrificing themselves to themselves; then to compound the silliness, they raise the dead sacrifice back from the dead anyway, now no longer grumpy but a divine happy-chappy!

O, what a tangled web we weave, when first we practise to deceive . . . ourselves: this counterfeit Gospel is, yes, a tangled web of fatal misapprehensions about God, the Kingdom, salvation, sin, life itself, which has its roots deep in pre-incarnation human history, emerged almost immediately after Jesus left for parts unknown, and has held the Christian church captive in one way or another right down to the present day. What a disaster! In fact, as we will see in the next chapter, it is really only *in spite of* itself—in spite of its becoming, as we've just seen, a little kingdom unto itself, a worldly, institutionalised, exclusive salvation gatekeeper—that the church has made any headway at all in carrying out its originally intended task of being a pilot-project for a true Kingdom of love and grace. And along the way, unfortunately, *because of* itself and the wrong direction it headed off on almost from the beginning, the church has caused much real harm in the world—more harm than good, I am sure you will lose no time in telling me!

A true Kingdom: the focus of the true, incarnational Gospel is not on an otherworldly future but a this-worldly present, on humanity making the transition, now, from natural selfishness to very unnatural selflessness, on individual believers and the collective of the church being a pilot-project for a whole world transformed. So utterly unnatural that no effort or works of our own to stimulate or simulate it will ever work. We have rehearsed this already: only faith in an invisible God of love can get us, humanity, over the line. But by surrendering to its own fears and pride—the very opposite of faith—the church fabricated a counterfeit Gospel of its own and sold it to the hungry, gullible masses of the world, allying itself, in the process, with worldly power. So much for pilot-project of a transformed world!

In the story of the Kingdom coming and the pilot-project for it we have made it now as far as the fourth century CE, the time of Constantine then Augustine. The pilot-project is faltering, to say the least: early experiments in democracy have been overwhelmed by Roman imperial power, and the church has gone off on the unhelpful tangent we've just described, turning itself, in the process, into an enemy of democratic development. Let's now see what happened next.

A Forum for Theology in the World Vol 12 No 1/2025

Chapter 8
The Gospel Strikes Back

A God who doesn't exist and a counterfeit Gospel: the two go together quite nicely, don't you think?! We are back at the beginning of Chapter 4, in fact, where all our problems started—it's as if the incarnation hadn't actually happened! Normally Christians look back on the deal struck by the church and Roman Emperor Constantine in early fourth century CE as a triumph—no more persecutions now, yay!—but in fact it was a disaster, setting back the cause of the pilot-project for a Kingdom coming perhaps by a millennium or more. Of course, however, it did happen—the incarnation—and because of that, and, yes, despite the way the church was developing, the real transformation that was beginning to occur in individual believers' lives and in the lives of Christian communities kept on pushing through.

The two things, individual life and life in community, are inextricably linked, for all the reasons we've rehearsed in previous chapters of this book. Remember, what is driving this whole movement is a profound evolutionary pressure, operating at the deepest level of human experience, a pressure to develop the ways and means of cooperating together, consciously, intentionally, creatively, in order first just to survive, then to hopefully thrive. At the individual level—now we're back in Chapter 2—this pressure manifests as what we described as *psychological necessity*, a deep inner urge to connect with others, to be liked, loved, accepted, approved of by others, to not be alone, to connect with life, with the world, the cosmos, ultimately—now that we have reluctantly accepted there really must be such an entity—with the invisible God of love.

Connect with others, and eventually with the whole cosmos and God: the central focus of human life is on relationships and community, in other words, as we keep saying. Jesus didn't come to save individuals by giving them a ticket each to a happy afterlife; no, he came to save communities, to transform our common life together, a transformation that will eventually, if all goes according to plan, encompass the whole of humanity. There is the beautiful image of the transformed community, continually growing and reaching out to the world, expressed in typically parabolic form by Jesus, as a fruit-bearing vine:

> I am the true vine . . . Remain in me, as I also remain in you. No branch can bear fruit by itself; it must remain in the vine. Neither can you bear fruit unless you remain in me . . . I am the vine; you are the branches. If you remain in me and I in you, you will bear much fruit; apart from me you can do nothing . . . If you remain in me and my words remain in you, ask whatever you wish, and it will be done for you . . . that you bear much fruit, showing yourselves to be my disciples.[1]

'Abiding in the vine', so goes the old Gospel song: we are allowing ourselves to be, so to speak, grafted into a new community, onto a new host organism, almost, a new life source. Our deep urge for connection, which first manifests itself as a selfish desire to win the approval of others by impressing them with the 'good works' we do, by manipulating or controlling them in some way, begins to be transformed into something new, a new natural to replace the old one. We start finding the strength, the courage, to let go of our need for approval—which can never really be satisfied anyway—and imaginatively, selflessly project ourselves into the shoes and minds of others, trying to understand their needs and wants; then we act accordingly. This new habit, new way of living, becomes more and more natural—but only as we remain, abide in the vine, continuing to draw on the vitalizing energy it provides.

And all of us are capable of such selflessness in some degree, by the way, because of how the world has developed, not just since the incarnation itself, but because of how the invisible God's 'plan of salvation' has unfolded through the entirety of human history. We are definitely going over old ground here, but it is a point worth labouring: the real impact of the transformation in question, from selfishness

---

1. Jhn 15:1–8 (NIV).

to selflessness, is foremostly on communities, not individuals. A transformation from power-based, hierarchical communities, as we have been saying, to truly democratic communities based on selfless love, on faith in an invisible God.

This point worth labouring, you might be able to see, is tautological—after all, you cannot practise selflessness without other selves to practise it on! This was the impulse that kept on pushing through, despite what the church was becoming: the impulse for freedom, for breaking free from oppressive rulers and structures, both worldly and spiritual, for building free democratic communities based on selfless cooperation. So, as the church develops beyond the original communities we described at the start of last chapter, seeming to go, as we noted, in precisely the reverse direction, it is confronted, as we will see now, by a constant counter movement of dissenting and innovating voices. Yes, it is an often-bloody spectacle of suppressions and persecutions of allegedly heretical individuals and groups, continual schisms and breakaways, but in spite of or perhaps because of all the carnage, the true Kingdom we are looking for keeps growing in its own inimitable and ineluctable way.

Augustine himself, after seeing off the pagan Manichee's, had to deal next with the heretical Donatists and Pelagians.[2] During the fifth century CE the so-called Church of the East and the Oriental Orthodox Churches break away from Rome; then in 1054, the Great Schism occurs and the Eastern Orthodox Churches go their own way. In 1517 the amazing figure of Martin Luther bursts onto the scene and the Protestant Reformation is born, but the reform movement itself splits almost immediately into at least four streams: Lutheran, Reformed, Anabaptist and Anglican. By the time we get to the twentieth century with the explosion of Pentecostalism and charismatic Christianity, schism, breakaway, renewal become the norm, with a seemingly endless search for authentic, back-to-roots

---

2. The original Donatists were Carthaginian schismatics in fourth and fifth century, but Donatism eventually became the charge of choice levelled by the mainstream church of the day, Roman or Protestant, against individuals or groups who protested immorality and corruption in the church hierarchy. Pelagius was a British ascetic and philosopher, opposed by Augustine for his unorthodox views on human nature and free will, who later gave his name to the accusation—Pelagianism—levelled against just about anyone who dared question orthodox church doctrine.

expressions of Christian faith—for what we have described as the original, true Gospel. What started out as an amazing quest for unity, community, Kingdom, is now, in the twenty-first century, divided into a dizzying, ever-expanding array of separate denominations and churches, all competing for what seems to be, at least in the west, a dwindling market of interested believers.

As long as the focus is first on making sure we get to heaven when we die, the true Gospel will always elude the church's best efforts to find it and live it. Thus, Luther himself, even though he rediscovered the amazing truth of *sola fide*, 'by faith alone', and successfully exposed the very sophisticated and corrupt works program the Roman Church had become, still wanted a unified, state-enforced hierarchical church, and if it couldn't be a universal one controlled ultimately by the emperor, then please let it be at least a national one. Yes, the emperor or local ruler might be corrupt and oppressive, but the grace that is coming to you regardless, through your faith, will have its real pay-off in the next life, if not in this one.

In the twentieth century Luther's famous successor Dietrich Bonhoeffer—pastor, theologian and conspirator, eventually hung for opposing what the German state had then become under the Nazis—spoke out against the false, counterfeit notion of 'cheap grace'.[3] For Bonhoeffer, grace is, rather, potentially costly, for this life now not the next, for selfless works that help to make the world a better place and might cost you something now, your life even. The works will not save you because you are already saved by your faith, but through them you can do something much more important: participate in the exciting, risky task of building God's Kingdom on earth now, which might include, where necessary, opposing the corrupt cities and kingdoms of this world.

In fact, it was often the dissenting individuals and groups who led the charge for a transformed Kingdom of this world, keeping the original pilot-project going despite the institutional church's best attempts to suppress them or wipe them out. Persecuted by the Roman Church or the various state churches, they were forced to either set up their own closed dissenting communities within existing states, or flee as refugees and migrants to the 'New World'.

---

3. See Dietrich Bonhoeffer, *The Cost of Discipleship* [1937], English translation by RH Fuller (London: SCM Press, 1948).

The many dissenting groups who migrated to North America in the sixteenth and seventeenth century, for example, were instrumental in the American Revolution, a remarkable event which was as much about separation from the tyranny of the state established Church of England as it was from that of the British crown. Finally, in the newly minted American republic, we have full separation between church and state, religious toleration, and a completely secular democracy with a constitution which mentions God precisely nowhere. It's an amazing price to pay: the greenback might claim 'In God We Trust', but it is a God we officially no longer believe in, let alone trust, our old friend the God who doesn't exist!

So, God is now officially out of the equation, which means that, despite the fact that the ideals of the world's first fully-fledged democracy—unity, justice, peace, equality, freedom and so on—look suspiciously like the ideals the primitive church aspired to, there is now one important thing fatally missing: the God of love, faith in whom alone makes such an unnatural community of human individuals even possible, let alone gives it half a chance of working. That faith was still there, of course, along with the God of love in question, and because of it the republic established itself as a democracy rather than a new form of tyranny, something subsequent major revolutions failed to achieve, as we will note shortly. But to pull off the miracle the revolutionaries were forced to boot the other God—the one who actually didn't exist—out of the country with his collaborator, the hated King George! The baby was thrown out with the bathwater, you'd be tempted to say, the right God with the wrong one.

Are you losing track of which God is which here? I hope so! Or which Gospel is which? In fact, it was the counterfeit version of the Gospel—the one that set its sights on an otherworldly kingdom—that the revolutionaries were forced to reject, in order to set forth on the task of building what was essentially the first substantial Kingdom of this world, even if the God whose Kingdom it actually was rated no mention in its founding document—and even if the kingdom in question was actually a republic! You might even say that the pilot-project we've been speaking about at this point effectively passed over from the church, which had long since repudiated it anyway, to the American state. 'God bless America!', I can hear you intoning ironically right now.

'We hold these truths to be self-evident, that all men are created equal . . .',[4] and so on and so forth. Well, it is not self-evident, and the idea of it only popped into the revolutionaries' heads because of the teachings and amazing works of a certain Jesus of Nazareth some seventeen centuries before their time. *In*equality, in fact, is the self-evident, natural norm of humanity. Yes, slavery was still widely accepted and practised at the time of the revolution, the final dispossession of native Americans was still to come, and women had to wait another 150 years to gain theoretical equality with men; but it was still a genuine pilot-project of a Godly polity on earth. Again, however, as the republic has continued to develop to this day, and even when Christian believers have been at the forefront of positive social change, as they often have, it has largely been despite the established institutional churches with their typically conservative agendas. I'm thinking of those who led the fight against slavery in the US, for example, or were instrumental in the civil rights movement, the individuals and groups in whom the impetus of the original, true Gospel kept, as we have described it, pushing through.

But, yes, fatally missing, the God who no longer exists. You might say that the birth of modern atheism was in the American revolution. Or was it in the European Enlightenment, or the Scientific Revolution, or the Reformation, or the Renaissance even; or even, as we suggested in Chapter 4, in the mythical Garden back in the day—lost, in point of fact, in the indeterminate sands of evolutionary time, because, well, as we've noted, the whole Garden episode didn't literally happen anyway. Subsequent major revolutions—French, Russian then Chinese—were more intentionally atheistic, and the existing tyrannies that were overthrown in each case were replaced by even worse ones, the Russian and Chinese people still waiting to this day for the great and just kingdom of this world their respective revolutionary leaders promised.

The next dissenters were the so-called liberal philosophers and theologians from the seventeenth century onwards, and beyond them the great atheist, humanist heroes of the modern era, all intent on, in their different ways, shooting down in flames the counterfeit Gospel the church had been busily constructing all those centuries past. Marx, for example, blew the whistle on the historic collusion between

---

4. *The Declaration of Independence* of The Thirteen United States of America, July 4, 1776.

organised religion and the ruling classes, keeping the masses of the poor doped up on belief in a God who would give them final succour only beyond the grave, provided they followed the rules now—the famous 'opium of the people'.

No religion, no God at all, eventually, is better than a false one who turns you into a mere cog in the capitalist-industrial machine. Or maybe not? We are back in a 'state of nature', in the anarchy of our evolutionary past, where only the strong survive, back in the Garden thinking we can do better on our own anyway. The final elimination of the God who doesn't exist in the diatribes of the French revolutionaries, Marx, Nietzsche and eventually Freud, unleashed multiple reigns of terror, the horrors of Stalinism, Nazism and Fascism: we must take control of our own destiny, against the *Ancien Regime*, the Tsars, or whoever, against the weakness of our own servile human nature, against God above all!

Marx decisively put the old, fake gospel to the sword, but only to replace it with a new fake one, complete with its own version of the Kingdom, the so-called 'workers' paradise', an amazing future state of society in which all people will be equal and free and the state will wither away, having completed its job—of demolishing the old hegemony of the ruling classes and capital—and thereby rendering itself redundant. Yes! It is a beautiful vision, and Marx worked so hard in the middle period of his life to promote a democratic way forward against the wearying resistance of hegemonic nineteenth century Prussia and the German people so long in a state of abject compliance. But then his vision was hijacked by the ones who were less patient, more determined to make things happen by fair means or foul, more ruthlessly, egotistically motivated, Lenin, Stalin and Mao foremost among them, others following in their wake.

Yes, the power of the old regimes must be broken down somehow, none more so than the old natural human regime of selfishness, the great cultural hegemon of taking care of number one and hang the rest—but only faith in an invisible God of love can do that, as we've seen. Faith in human nature, in humans coming good once you set them free from their political and religious bonds, is a recipe for disaster, for anarchy, which only a new 'strong-man' authoritarianism can cure—hence Napoleon after the revolution, Hitler after the political and economic chaos of the Weimar republic, and more recently Putin after the collapse of the Soviet Union, megalomaniac saviours of the people one and all.

Marx's radical deconstruction of the evils of the industrial revolution and capitalist political economy eventually bore fruit, not in the places where it was violently transplanted, but back home in the western democracies, with gradual social, political and economic reform, the rise of trade unionism and the development of modern social democracy and the welfare state—thank you Karl! But again, we're throwing the baby out with the bathwater, the God who does exist along with the one who doesn't. By the time we get to the twenty-first century with the increasing political polarization and polycrisis we started our journey with, the Marxist vision has become a new form of intellectual and spiritual hegemony on a par with the counterfeit Gospel it hoped to displace, now a profoundly polarizing influence.

The liberal philosophers and theologians, such iconic figures as Descartes, Spinoza, Rousseau, Locke, Kant, Hegel, Strauss and, more recently, Bultmann, Tillich, Spong, Fox and Borg, were reacting to the rise of modern science, the amazing cultural phenomenon which more than anything else, as we saw early on, gave birth to modern atheism and humanism. By the early nineteenth century, it was becoming increasingly evident that science, rather than the church or Jesus, would turn out to be the real saviour of humankind. The liberals rejected the authority of church tradition in favour of scientific reason and experience: no longer could we countenance a transcendent, absolutist God *out there*, controlling everything by divine fiat. If there was to be any God at all, they could only be one who was immanent, *inside* of us, a life force or vital energy, perhaps, 'the ground of being' as Tillich described it.[5] A God of love, yes, not judgement, who will save us by setting us free from the false consciousness of sin the traditional church has hooked us on—free to be our true selves and through doing so solve all the problems of the world ourselves, through hard work, social reform and, of course, especially, science. It was a repudiation of not just original sin but sin altogether, so that we no longer needed a God above to forgive us and give us a ticket to the happy afterlife—an irrational notion, anyway, unacceptable in the new age of science.

---

5. See, for example, Paul Tillich, *Systematic Theology, Volume 1* (Chicago: University of Chicago Press, 1973).

Liberalism is the child of science and the Enlightenment, confident in human reason, individualistic, progressive in outlook; but if the horrors of the twentieth century did not finally quench its optimism, our current polycrisis surely does. Like modern atheism it replaces the old counterfeit Gospel with a new one. Yes, it certainly sets its sights on a good and just Kingdom of this world, and along with the atheistic liberalism of the political left, inspired by Marx, liberal Christianity has had a profoundly positive impact on the development of social democracy in the west and around the globe, confronting the worst impacts of colonialism, absolutism, imperialism, racism, sexism and so on. But the price it has paid is the same: the new God it constructed to replace the old one is one who barely exists, a disempowered, non-interventionist God existing only faintly on the margins of life. The incarnation itself—the birth, death and resurrection of Jesus—is no longer a unique, explicit, historical intervention, rather, in more recent progressive Christian accounts, for example, an abstract, general, natural principle of life-death-rebirth.

At the worst, by eliminating sin, liberalism is forced to put its hopes in the essential goodness of human nature—if only we can get over all the guilty hang-ups about sin the traditional church has foisted on us! It's an appealing but dangerous fantasy, cutting us off from the real truth about ourselves, that we are naturally, habitually, sinfully selfish. In reality, as we've seen, only outside intervention of the order of the incarnation by a God who really does exist can bring about the inner transformation required—from natural selfishness to unnatural selflessness—to save us from self-destruction.

By the early twentieth century liberalism was becoming mainstream, institutionalized, middle class, academic—well-intentioned, no doubt, but in self-exile from the real power-source that could change the lives of individuals, communities and societies. So, as if on cue, we get the counter-reaction explosion of Pentecostalism and charismatic Christianity, first in the US then spreading rapidly around the globe, now with huge congregations in Africa, Latin America and Asia. About one in twelve human beings on the planet are now Pentecostal or charismatic, but the roots of the movement lie much earlier, at least as far back as the so-called Radical Reformation of the sixteenth century—no sooner had Luther published his famous 95 theses in Germany in 1517, than fanatical groups such as the Zwickau prophets and Anabaptists emerged, rebelling against both church and state authority. The mainstream reformation of Luther, Zwingli and Calvin emphasized the primacy of scripture over church tradition, but for the radicals even this was too much; they wanted direct experience, straight from God, unmediated, unvarnished. Dramatic signs, prophecies, visions, miracles, healings, speaking in strange tongues—these were all things people in Jesus' day experienced, so why not us now? And that is exactly what the Pentecostals and charismatics have sought in their revivals of the last hundred years.

The staid, quiet devotion of the middle class, mainstream church, with a retiring, ineffectual God, seemingly absent from the grind of ordinary life, just will not cut it when you are poor, sick, living on the margins, the whole world seems to be against you. The poor and marginalized in western countries, the endless poor in developing countries, desperately seeking new life, a better life: it is these people who are especially drawn to the Pentecostal revolution. The revivals are marked by charismatic preachers and healers operating outside organized church supervision, part prophet, part showman, often eventually exposed as hucksters, abusers, drunks. Why does this happen? In the twenty-first century the hallmark of Pentecostalism is wonderfully upbeat, soulful pop music, building the faithful up into an emotional frenzy before all the preaching, healing and converting begins. It is a socially conservative, individualistic Gospel: the focus is always on me, my experience, a better, happier, more prosperous life for me now, and, yes, even more importantly, an assured happy life beyond the grave, a ticket to heaven for me, me, me. So—to answer the question—the rock star preachers, mediating these feelgood emotional experiences, are in constant danger of getting caught up in their own hype and turning into narcissistic manipulators. In the end, beyond the emotion and hype, beyond the communities which swell rapidly into mega-churches then splinter suddenly into breakaways, it is, nevertheless, another counterfeit version of the Gospel.

Yes, the initial powerful shock medicine of suddenly being in real community, surrounded by people who don't judge you, just care for you and offer you hope for a better life: it is an amazing injection of real agency into the life of people disempowered and marginalized by mainstream society, a potential ticket out of loneliness, addiction, poverty. But no, as we have noted, the salvation offered by the Gospel is not primarily for me to have a nice experience, a better life; but for me to learn some selflessness, the benefit of which goes out into community and society, and only incidentally benefits me, myself—and in fact might lead to significant disbenefit, real suffering, even death, for me. The faithful are sold something completely real—a God who loves them unconditionally—at the same time as something completely false, a false notion of what that love is for. The signs and wonders, the miracle healings, the direct experience of the Spirit unmediated by the community of believers, are not what the true Gospel offers. They might seem to work in the moment, but that is just a rush of hope, of agency, of 'positive thinking', and when the initial rush wears off, you'll be heading out the backdoor quietly, losing a faith that seemed so real but turned out an illusion, or moving on to the next new Pentecostal ministry that offers itself to you, in vain hope of the real thing, finally, next time.

The other reaction against the mainstream church in the twentieth century was the 'liberation theology' movement, developing in the Latin American Catholic Church from the 1960's onwards. The movement's leaders aimed to focus the attention of the church on social inequality and injustice, presenting a Marxist-like critique of institutionalized, systemic sin and evil under the frequently corrupt right-wing regimes of the region, with whom the mainstream conservative church was often in cahoots. Criticized by Rome for their challenge to traditional church authority and for their sympathy with Marxist thought—even to the extent of in some cases directly supporting Marxist political and guerilla movements—the focus was on supporting the poor to organize into new communities based on justice and equality, for mutual protection and care, over and against corrupt central states which typically only exploited the poor.

The original Latin American movement has spawned other liberation theologies since the 1960s, for example black theology in North America, Dalit theology in India, Palestinian liberation theology, as well as theologies associated with marginalized groups such as queer theology for LGBTQ+ Christians. But even though these theologies challenge real cultural structures of sin, they do so at the expense of acknowledging individual sin and personal responsibility. Individuals are seen as innocent victims of the sin that is entirely in the culture or system around, and liberation is, therefore, not from our own naturally sinful selves, but from the sinful system and culture that oppresses us. Yes, the Kingdom *is* a liberation of culture and society from sinful structures, but the primary medium of this is individual liberation—not from these external structures first, but from our natural inner state of selfish sinfulness. It's a counterfeit Gospel again: we can save ourselves by our own works, by activism to achieve our own rights, by taking control over our own lives, by discovering or creating our natural, sin-free personal identity that has hitherto been suppressed by "the system".

Beyond liberalism and Pentecostalism, beyond the church altogether in fact, we have, finally, the so-called 'New Age' spirituality movement, emerging in western countries from the 1960s onwards. 'I'm not religious, I'm spiritual' is the common claim, but it's a rejection not of religion in general, rather of organized Christianity in particular, the movement frequently dabbling in eastern religions, especially Buddhism, and traditional indigenous religions from various parts of the globe. In the west the spirituality movement is typically countercultural, anti-establishment, focussing, like Pentecostalism and liberalism, on individual spiritual experience and wellbeing over and against mainstream religious and secular culture which, allegedly, constantly frustrate the individual's journey of self-discovery and realization.

Again, there is so much good, so much help for struggling, disaffected individuals—for all of us, in fact—in the rediscovery and development of many traditional spiritual practices. But the spirituality movement in general is, nevertheless, very much a sort of neo-gnosticism, a counterfeit Gospel of its own, positing as it does an intrinsically harmful world-system—western capitalist-consumerist-scientific-industrial society and culture—which can, however, be transcended through personal effort based on particular sorts of secret knowledge that have been suppressed or lost but now rediscovered. There is certainly no focus on the transformation of communities and societies through individual transformation from selfishness to selflessness that the true Gospel inspires. In the end the movement is socially conservative, or even regressive, calling as it sometimes does for a return to older pre-modern, pre-democratic social forms.

You can see, at any rate, that even though liberal or (as it is now often called) progressive Christianity, in its various forms, on one hand, and Pentecostal and charismatic Christianity on the other, are poles apart, opposing ends of the very wide spectrum of modern Christianity, what they have in common is that they are both all about *me*: what I can do, what experiences I can have, how I can change my own life and/or the world through my own efforts and works; what personal benefits I can receive, now and/or in the next life, if I play my cards right. In the language of the reformers, therefore, both constitute 'works programs', attempts to 'save' yourself and/or the world by your own efforts and actions. Both erect for themselves a new counterfeit Gospel, and both cut themselves off from the real source of power, the Gospel power to transform individuals and communities, to transform this present world into a Kingdom of justice and peace, a true kingdom of heaven on earth.

So, yes, as we have noted, the pilot-project of the amazing Kingdom to come, inaugurated by the enigmatic Jesus of Nazareth, the hopeful fruition point to which human life is evolving, effectively passed over from the church to the modern, secular, democratic sphere sometime around the American revolution, in doing so freeing itself from the constraints of the old order of autocratic, hierarchical church and state, but at the same time jettisoning the real power to make it happen, the real God whom, as we have discovered, existed all along and was always our only hope for survival, for avoiding complete self-destruction—throwing out the baby with the bathwater, as we have expressed it, the helpful God who does exist along with the very unhelpful one who doesn't.

Where is it now, the pilot-project, as I write and you read? By 2024 democracy had developed in the world to the extent that over four billion people, more than half the total world population, voted in elections sometime during the year. Yet now we seem to be in polycrisis mode—the point at which we started this tale—with threats to democracy everywhere and a profound loss of faith in it in the west. At same time the church in the west, with numbers dwindling alarmingly across all mainstream denominations, is lost in endless debate and agonizing over its own survival, no pilot-project in sight—if indeed it had ever grasped that essential nature of its God-given mission in the world! What, then, is the way forward from here—what indeed does the invisible God of love have up their sleeve for us next? Well, it is time now to dust off our crystal balls and see what the future of this mighty illusion—the God who doesn't exist but actually does—could possibly be.

Chapter 9
Reality Itself

A God who doesn't exist and a counterfeit Gospel: out of desperation, and pride, out of our natural self-centredness and over-weening self-belief, we created them both—as we saw in Chapters 7 and 8. And now we've rejected them: good riddance to bad rubbish on both counts, I say! But, shock-horror, now we have no God at all anymore, 'no hell below us, above us only sky', as John Lennon sings. We're stone motherless on our own.

Like Adam and Eve back in the day, as we have rehearsed, this is how it happens in our lives: we wake up one morning—we might be late in our teen or even our autumn years—and realize that oh, by the way, God does not exist anymore—come to think of it, never did, obviously! I am on my own, basically, accountable to myself alone, I can do anything I want, no-one can tell me what to do. A great burden disappears, a weight of guilt and condemnation, I'm free, a little flutter of hope stirs within my breast, I drag myself out of bed and up into the day.

But it doesn't last long—the great 'I am'. Pretty soon we realise that this cosmic aloneness is the night-terror of our deepest childhood, which our parents first rescued us from, channelling the God who actually does exist—acting *in loco dei*, as we have described it—with their selfless, comforting love. Now, however, we certainly are on our own, either because we have consciously rejected our parents, or because they are just not around anymore. We might be in a great relationship, have lots of family close-by, plenty of good friends and life in the community—but our ability to sustain all these relationships is entirely dependent on our capacity to generate a little selfless love ourselves, at least now and again, which we can never find within ourselves unless we have previously had it planted there from the outside, ultimately from and by the invisible God of love, acting through our parents, through the culture around us—as we have also rehearsed, repeatedly.

No, there is no running from the reality of it—although the thrill might last for a while, we might be cursed by success; and drugs too, administered judiciously or even recklessly, might delay the moment—no, the self-sufficient, self-enclosed self who seems to exist, apart from the God who doesn't, is not only the greatest of all delusions, but the cause of all human ills, of all the anxiety about life we feel, of the living hell we create for ourselves when we choose to live in this way, which is really only a shadow of the more permanent cosmic aloneness that awaits us beyond physical death if we don't pull ourselves out of the spiral before it's too late. Hells bells! Help!

Well, help has come, has always been there, will always be there, as we have seen. Being an illusion, it is remarkably easy to dispel: pop! there it goes! The hell we fear might come upon planet earth in the next little while—the polycrisis with which we launched this book, the downfall of democracy, economic collapse, environmental emergency, species extinction, dystopia, the existential anxiety about all this that consumes us—is really a figure, an echo of that deepest night terror and fear of ultimate aloneness that lurks and has always lurked within the human psyche, right from the beginning, whenever that was. So, it is a phantom, an illusion too.

This is not to downplay in any way the extent and difficulty of the challenges we face. Quite the contrary, acknowledging our powerlessness to deal with these challenges and prevent the worst from happening is precisely the place we need to be in, the beginning of their resolution and the journey to the great future we all long for. As much as we feel the fear of night terror and little old me being entirely alone and separate and powerless in this giant indifferent cosmos, we also, as that delusion-bubble bursts in the morning with our parents love and the renewal of connection with the people and culture around us, sense the amazing hope of an open, exciting, positive future that awaits, in a cosmos that is not indifferent to us but has at its centre a God who really exists and is the ultimate source of love and transcendence. Faith and trust in that God, obedience to their call to live and love selflessly, to care for, respect and serve others and the world—it is a winning formula!

The challenges we face: well might we tremble at their intractability if it is just up to us to solve them—but that, of course, our trying to do it on our own, is the cause of all our problems in the first place. Our contemporary rejection of God distorts our understanding of the problems, making them seem intractable, insoluble, when in fact they are practical problems amenable to practical solutions, if and when we find, together, the right heart with which to approach them.

Distorted understanding: let us begin our crystal ball gazing into potential futures by exploring, and deconstructing, the great dystopian visions of the present day. Once we have them out of the way, we might be able to see more clearly the positive future that is really coming towards us, the coming to fruition of the amazing Kingdom foretold and inaugurated by the inimitable Jesus of Nazareth all those years ago.

Dystopian visions: here is the mother of them all, the modern scientific one, written on a plaque beside a model astrolabe on top of the dam wall at Mt Lofty Botanic Gardens in Crafers, South Australia, part of an interpretive trail set up for visiting school children:

> Life on earth is only possible because of stars.
> Almost every element of earth was made inside a star.
> We feed off energy provided by our star, the sun,
> And one distant day we will be consumed by it.

Help! Initially you are astonished and dismayed by such a horrifying conception, inflicted on innocent children and casual Sunday strollers. But then you think, 'fair enough', because it is actually true—it has, does it not, the cast-iron warrant of science itself backing it up. Or does it?

The fabled 'heat death of the universe', now sometimes colourfully called the 'Big Chill' or 'Big Freeze': on one hand it is based on the simple observation that, sooner or later, fires go out when the fuel burning runs out, that cars stop when they run out of petrol. All you then need is a bit of imaginative extrapolation to catch a vision of our sun one day running out of nuclear fuel and burning out, swelling wildly, consuming our own planet and the whole solar system in its last dying gasps. Then the whole universe of stars and galaxies doing the same thing.

That is what we have to look forward to, the creators of the interpretive trail at Mt Lofty cheerfully tell the little kiddies and other passers-by. By latest estimates it might be 2–3 billion years in the future, it might be incredibly speculative, hypothetical, based on an outrageous extrapolation forward in time, but it is important for you to know, my little darlings. Why, you wonder? Because that is what science says, and science rules, science tells you what is really going on in the world; and, beyond this, by the way, there is no God, no heaven, no fairytale ending to the world, science alone is true, you'd better believe it. With our own efforts and especially with the help of science we can make a pretty good life for ourselves for a while; but, my darlings, don't delude yourselves with any of that phony-baloney religion stuff that there's any ultimate, long-term future for any of us.

Who's being paranoid here? Me, in my imaginative reconstruction of the thought patterns of the astrolabe trail creators, or the creators themselves in concocting such a nightmare vision in the first place?! The assumption here is that there is a fixed, finite amount of virtual or potential energy in the universe available to be converted into actual or kinetic energy which, being fixed and finite, will inevitably one day run out. The universe as a 'closed system' will consequently always tend toward maximum disorder or *entropy*, so that the day will come when no new kinetic energy can be generated, all heat will dissipate and it will be very cold indeed, absolute zero (−273.15°C) everywhere, everything absolutely, totally dead.

I am quoting here the famous Second Law of Thermodynamics, which, among other things, introduces this enigmatic concept of entropy to quantitatively measure the amount of disorder in a physical system. The Second Law is a scientific formalism that is amazingly handy in the design and operation of any sort of technology that involves heat transfer—fridges, air-conditioners, heat pumps and so on—but, as we are about to see, its extrapolation to the universe as a whole is another thing altogether, a giant overreach.

The universe as a closed system: the Second Law strictly only applies to finite physical systems that are closed off to matter or energy transfer, 100% insulated, from the outside world. Now, it is perfectly possible to build physical systems on a small scale that are close enough to 100% insulated for all practical purposes—that is where the law comes into its own—and, yes, if we imagine that the universe taken as a whole is finite, it is plausible to consider it as a closed physical system—at least in theory. But there's a potential very significant spanner in the works: *agency*.

You will remember agency from Chapter 3: the living agency of organisms, the general agency that gives rise to other organised structures around us, such as nuclei, atoms, stars, solar systems and galaxies. Agency can act within a physical system as an independent source of order—'from the outside', as we have described it, although not from spatially outside, rather from a reality that seems to exist prior to and independently of the physical system itself. Agency, in fact, some form or other of it, as we discussed in Chapter 3, generates both the physical matter and the virtual structure of any physical system. So, even if we could somehow guarantee that a physical system, even the universe as a whole, was 100% closed off from matter and energy transfer, we could never guarantee it was closed off from the action of agency.

The spanner in the works: agency can operate in reverse to entropy, increasing the order in systems in which it operates, defying the Second Law. Think, for example, of a conscientious parent tidying up a bedroom left in a disastrous state by their teenage child—the parent is a living agent, making the room more ordered and functional for future occupation and use by their child. Or geological processes that lead to the formation of highly ordered crystalline mineral structures such as quartz or diamond. Everywhere we look in our universe we see the action of various forms of agency increasing order, reversing entropy, for the short, medium, or sometimes very long term. Yes, as far as the agency of individual living organisms is concerned, we're always talking about a finite action: every organism dies eventually, and, apart from that, the actions of particular organisms are often decidedly entropic—the teenager in question above, for example, or an animal predator species unwittingly eating its prey species all the way to extinction. But organic life as a whole has just kept expanding on planet earth, evolving into ever newer and more sophisticated forms, multiplying everywhere it goes, even if things seem to be hanging in the balance right now in our time of polycrisis. So, there is no unequivocal indication yet that life itself is, necessarily, a finite source of order.

We have recently been forced to acknowledge the existence of the greatest agent of them all, at any rate—the invisible love-teaching God—so while particular finite closed physical systems might perforce go very close to obeying the Second Law, the universe as a whole has what we might well describe as a choice. Thus, for example, we human agents, remarkably consequential creatures that we are, might choose, against our natural selfish inclinations, to act selflessly in our relationships with others, increasing the order, harmony and functionality of the communities and societies in which we operate, working in reverse to the selfish, self-centred actions of some or many others; thereby, dare I say it, decreasing the overall entropy of the world. Selflessness, by a human agent, is, in these terms, a quintessential act of anti-entropy.

We will see this very clearly shortly, in relation to the current threat of global warming, the second in our list of dystopian visions. But I mean no metaphor here: the incarnation of Jesus of Nazareth 2000 years ago was an amazing injection of real agency into the world, agency to broker humanity's transition, as we have described it, from natural selfishness to unnatural selflessness, a transition which radically reverses the entropic tendencies of that historic natural selfishness. So, at any rate, because of the radical, unknown, potentially unlimited possibilities of agency generally, there is no inevitable heat death, Big Chill, hell itself freezing over—and if you come across children traumatised by the astrolabe trail at Mt Lofty Botanic Gardens, feel free to tell them what I have just said!

When we let go of the nightmare vision of heat death, we start to see the precise opposite happening everywhere in the universe: not a descent into chaos but an ascent into ever greater levels of order: more and more complexly structured organisms, ecosystems, biochemical systems, molecular, atomic and nuclear systems, geological and atmospheric systems, solar structures and systems, galactic systems, and so on. There seems to be no end to the intricate wonder of the cosmos; the more we find out about it, the more profoundly organized we realise it is. Yet all of this, or at least our part of it here on planet earth, now seems, somehow, to be terminally threatened.

Yes, the great dystopia of the moment, the beating heart of our present polycrisis: the terror of global warming and climate catastrophe. We referred to this nightmare scenario right at the outset of our tale: there seems to be no doubt, on the best evidence available, that accelerating burning of fossil fuels during the twentieth century has led to massive increases in carbon dioxide levels in the atmosphere and consequent global warming—leading, according to now very sophisticated climate prediction models, to significant and potentially harmful climate change. Even if a so-called 'tipping point' to catastrophic change is never reached, global warming will potentially cause significant social and economic disruption, threatening the future of many living species, including, obviously, humans.

At the same time, the solution seems to be readily at hand: rapidly accelerating development of renewable energy technology around the globe to gradually replace fossil fuels, reduce CO_2 emissions, and therefore avoid the worst consequences of rising global temperatures. In the meantime, other scientific, technological, social and economic innovation can help us adapt to changes in climate that are already occurring. Sounds pretty good; so, what's the problem, why are we so freaked out? Simply: we don't trust ourselves.

We don't trust ourselves for all the reasons we've rehearsed in this book. Humans are naturally selfish, and it is that selfishness that has got us into this nightmare scenario in the first place: indiscriminate burning of fossil fuels, to give us as much energy as we want, as cheaply as possible, hang the consequences for the future—the future is somebody else's problem, not mine. If individuals, corporations and governments around the world could just set aside their selfish concerns for once and cooperate on this one, we would be halfway there—but as if that is going to happen anytime soon?!

Some in the environmental movement imagine a 'great turning'[1] in which humanity moves from a mindset of control and exploitation of environmental resources to one of creative care and nurture, in doing so avoiding the looming climate disaster and building a sustainable long-term future for ourselves and the planet. A change in mindset, a radical shift in consciousness: proponents imagine that we will draw on the insights and practices of religious traditions from the past, and especially learn from indigenous cultures around the world, with their nurturing, sustaining, low-impact approaches to their environments. A third great revolution after the agricultural and industrial revolutions, recovering something essential we've lost in the process, a deep awareness of our need to live in harmony with nature, rather than at odds with it.

---

1. See the article by Joanna Macey at <https://www.ecoliteracy.org/article/great-turning>, accessed 19 November 2024. The concept first appeared in *The Great Turning* by David C Korten (USA: Berret-Koehler, 2018).

There's no doubt that, yes, we absolutely do need a big turnaround in our mindset to implement the solutions to destructive climate change now available quickly enough to avoid the worst. But how can that possibly occur? Somehow, we knew how to do it right in the past, and now we have to rediscover, recover that? Well, as we've noted, however, we didn't come out of a garden, out of a state of perfect harmony with nature: there never was a garden, and the mindset we are looking for is always a new thing in the world, never the recovery of an old thing.

The reality is that life has always been, right from the beginning, against the odds, an unrelenting pitched battle against a natural environment which is essentially hostile to it, and to survive long enough to reproduce life has had to find ways of controlling, harnessing and exploiting nature—no absolute equilibrium, balance or harmony possible; the best we (life) can ever hope for is a temporary truce. The harnessing of energy, its capture, storage and controlled release, is, as we saw in Chapter 3, the number one thing life has to master in order to survive. As cheaply as possible, hang the consequences: obviously the energy we expend in the activity of capture needs to be less in quantity than the energy we manage to capture, otherwise we are in trouble. Hopefully a lot less: if we chase prey all day but only occasionally make a catch, we won't last long, and we certainly won't have the energy to compete with other more successful members of our species over reproductive rights.

Homo sapiens is, now, yes, the first species to have been so successful in energy harnessing as to threaten not only its own future but the future of all life on the planet! But we are also the first species capable of reflecting on the perils of our success and making the smart decision to change our behaviour before it's too late. Yes, the solution is, indeed, for us to undergo a great turning—the word we used in Chapter 6 was *metanoia*, repentance, conversion, a complete change of mindset, made possible and only possible through outside intervention in our lives, courtesy of the God whom we've recently realized must have been there, existing and intervening, all along.

So, the solution has essentially already been provided. Part of this is certainly to draw on ancient spiritualities and environmental practices. The Hebrew Old Testament, as we discussed in Chapter 4, recounts a creation myth, the form of which was common throughout the ancient world: humans are created in God's image, specially fit for purpose to care for and nurture the whole of creation, to be caretakers, stewards of land, sea and sky. Precisely the same formulation occurs, for example, in Australian Aboriginal spirituality:

> Human beings are entrusted with the responsibility to cooperate with the Creator Spirit both to care for and to activate the life-forces within the land . . . The Creator Spirit is the true owner of the whole land and its waters . . . Aboriginal people know from the Creator Spirit, and from the land itself, that we are responsible for sustaining the land of Australia.[2]

But this task of stewardship has always been problematic, as history shows, because the creation stories were never literally true, we were not actually created fit for the purpose! Rather, we're evolved creatures, and while our unique self-consciousness gives us the potential to do the job of caretaking and stewardship, it also gives us the potential, as we have seen, to dominate, exploit and wreck the land, sea and sky on a scale never seen before in evolutionary history.

Let's not deceive ourselves: if the garden story had been literally true, if we really had started out in a garden, in a perfect state of harmony with the land as many or all the ancient creation stories depict, there would never have been a problem. Gardening for most of us is an enjoyable pastime, simple, relaxing, unproblematic. But the environmental reality we and all other organisms have had to adapt to and survive in has been the complete opposite: wild nature, treacherous, inimical to life, predators, unpredictable climate, danger almost everywhere we look, very, very problematic.

So, something more was always going to be needed to turn us into thoughtful and responsible stewards and caretakers, something new that comes into human life post the creation, much more recently in fact, as we have seen. To be effective stewards we need not just intelligence and know-how but the right heart attitude, the ability, as we've described it, to practise a little selflessness from time to time. So, yes, even though it has taken at least 150,000 years to reach a level that threatens the entire planet, our relationship with the land has always been problematic, and we've only relatively recently started to acquire the ability to do the job of caretaking and stewardship properly.

---

2. *Rainbow Spirit Theology: Towards and Australian Aboriginal Theology*, by the *Rainbow Spirit Elders*, Second Edition (Adelaide: ATF Press, 2007), 35–36.

We can see, therefore, that the radical shift in consciousness required to overcome the threat of climate change has already begun to occur, but what we now face is a new problem which threatens to derail the whole process—the very problem we identified at the start of this book. Thus, while we are right to hearken back to the traditional environmental practices of indigenous peoples around the globe, what we don't seem to want to do is take full cognizance of the fact that these practices were, without exception, inspired and informed by indigenous peoples' religious beliefs. No indigenous person ever claimed or claims to have decided to take a caring and nurturing approach to the environment off their own bat; the ability and inspiration to do so has always been ascribed to the particular deity, god or creator spirit whom the people interact with, acknowledge and worship. It's an amazing doublethink we impose on ourselves, in fact: we now tend to idolise traditional cultures and look to them for guidance and inspiration, all the while ignoring the fact that we have long since decided that any notion of gods, deities, ancestor spirits is a ridiculous and harmful fantasy!

So, yes, there is a mighty work of education and persuasion to be undertaken—to turn the global warming dreadnought around before it is too late. There may also be a place for direct, anti-democratic political action to attempt to coerce individuals, corporations and governments into changing their mindsets and practices, although such action seems more likely to just alienate the very people whose minds you are trying to change. But none of these on their own will ever be enough anyway. Activists demonize right-wing governments and corporations, 'big polluters' belching out greenhouse gases while raking in the profits, oblivious to the fact that the problem is much deeper and belongs to us all, and to the possibility that their own motivation is as self-centred and self-seeking as the other side, showing off their own virtue to contrast favourably with the vice of their opponents—all in a good cause, of course! Apart from faith and obedience, from listening carefully to and walking humbly with the God of love who, as we've seen, still exists, we are all basically on a self-destructive ego-trip, and this has been the human problem from the beginning, anyway, as we saw in Chapter 4, the cause of all subsequent problems including the big one we're trying to solve right now.

There is no escaping from it, I am sorry to say, we are just going to have to do it—if we want to avoid the worst, if our desire to save the world from the perils of global warming is at all genuine—re-admit the God who doesn't exist back into existence, humble ourselves, get down off our high horses, confess our own complicity, commit ourselves to our own great turning first. The same is true for all the other entropic, dystopian perils we rehearsed at the beginning of this book: threats to democracy, the rise of authoritarian states, nuclear or biological Armageddon, the potential triumph of the robots. But make sure you get the right God: not the fake one with their counterfeit Gospel whom you have most recently very rightly repudiated; rather the true one, the God of love and grace who, all the available evidence avers, as we've seen, was the only one who ever really existed anyway.

There now remains just one more dystopian bubble to burst, the oldest and most persistent one, before we finally get to some utopian dreaming. The fearful idea that it is only through the world experiencing some cataclysmic destructive future event that God will finally save us all, and create a new world, an elysian paradise, in which we will all live happily ever after—at least those of us righteous people who qualify. The unfortunate rest—they deserve it really—will be cast into an anti-paradise, hell, Hades, Sheol, a terrifying underworld where there will be 'weeping and wailing and gnashing of teeth'.[3]

Apocalypse, the end of the world—help! This is the God of judgement and punishment: humans are basically bad, mired in sin, God is allowing all this to play out in the world, sin and evil will triumph, then God will either allow the world to self-destruct or destroy it themselves, the good people—usually a small remnant—will go forward to paradise, the bad ones to hell.

The Christian version of cataclysmic apocalypse is based largely on the final book of the New Testament, the 'Book of Revelation' or 'Apocalypse of John'. The John in question is popularly assumed to be the same John who wrote the Gospel, one of Jesus' original disciples, but scholarly opinion holds to a different John, a Christian prophet living after the time of Jesus.[4] The book is an account, written some sixty years after Jesus' death, of a series of ecstatic visions John claimed

---

3. An expression that appears seven times in the New Testament, although how the 'wailing' slipped into the popular version historically is unknown.
4. In fact, the view of a different John dates from as early as the third century CE, with the African bishop Dionysius.

to have had while exiled on the Greek island of Patmos. Apocalyptic writing also appears in the Hebrew Old Testament, in the books of the prophets Joel, Zechariah and especially Isaiah and Daniel, and Jesus himself seems to wax apocalyptic in one particular passage that appears in three of the four Gospels, the so-called Olivet Discourse.[5]

Islam has a similar version of apocalypse, likewise depicting a final 'great tribulation' and 'day of judgement'. The earliest known version of apocalypse comes from the ancient Persian religion of Zoroastrianism, around the ninth century BCE, which imagines a great final battle between the forces of good and evil, reminiscent of the so-called 'Battle of Armageddon' described in the Book of Revelation.

It may well be that, psychologically speaking, such visions reflect the common, natural, very understandable human fear, which we surely all fall prey to sometimes, that the selfishness and malice within the human heart, and the real evil that seems to exist 'out there', are so intrinsically powerful that whatever goodness there might be in the world will never be enough to overcome them. This is certainly true of our current fears of, for example, 'climate apocalypse' and 'nuclear Armageddon'—channelling images directly from the New Testament book in question.

When will the apocalypse happen? 'Truly I tell you, this generation will certainly not pass away until all these things have happened',[6] says Jesus in the Olivet Discourse, describing dramatic events apparently soon to occur: 'For then there will be great distress, unequalled from the beginning of the world until now—and never to be equalled again.'[7] The answer is any day now, the end of the world seems always just about to come, anytime our lives and things around us start looking terrible, back in those days when life was much shorter and nastier, and especially now when, perhaps, moral decadence is rife, or the sky might be about to literally fall in due to climate change or nuclear emergency.

We're dealing with what has traditionally been an extremist view, for a long time the province of crackpots, fundamentalists, crazy religious sects the world over, but joined now by the more reasoned,

---

5. On the Mount of Olives in East Jerusalem: Lk 21, Mk 13, Matt 24–25.
6. Matt 24:34.
7. Matt 24:21.

rational view of contemporary apocalypticists, predicted on the basis of the best scientific evidence or political analysis available, although no longer with the prospect of a God who exists to save the day in the end. 'Jesus will solve climate change', the banner outside a church in Adelaide recently claimed, as reported to me by an acquaintance. I am sure the folks had in mind some sort of post-apocalyptic intervention, but there's an amazing (and different) sense in which it's actually true—as I will explain to you now.

The reference in fact is to the *Parousia*, the fabled Second Coming of Christ. Even in the Zoroastrian account there is a saviour figure, the *Saoshyant*,[8] who arrives after the last battle to bring about the resurrection of the dead in time for judgement day, although this is the mysterious, divine figure in question's first and only, rather than second, coming. Our own saviour, messiah, promises to return one day, and, yes, he always seems to do so in the context of a warning about trouble and tribulation to come for the believers. But hang on, wasn't his work of salvation, his defeat of the power of sin and selfishness over human life, completed back then, and the amazing kingdom of God on earth inaugurated? Why, when he has been busily announcing this Kingdom about to come, and performing all sorts of lovely miracles which are supposedly signs of it, will it be necessary for the Messiah to return one day to save us a second time?

It is an amazing contradiction, and the reason why belief in a terrible apocalypse followed by a literal second coming is typically the realm of crackpots and fundamentalists rather than the mainstream church, though the latter are the ones now more likely to believe in a non-religious apocalypse caused by climate change or nuclear conflict. No one, it seems, neither conservative nor progressive, finds themselves able to believe in anything good coming of this present world, let alone a growing Kingdom of love and peace and hope advanced on now 2000 years from its inauguration. Go figure!

We have rehearsed at length how we've arrived at this current impasse in human history, especially how the apparent disappearance of God in the contemporary world is both symptom and cause of our woes—no wonder we are terrified, if our saviour was always only a figment of our imagination! Jesus' strange warnings only add fuel to the fire, as if he himself had doubts and fears about the efficacy of

---

8. Literally, in Avestan, the old Persian language, 'one who brings benefit'.

what he was about to undertake, as if our saviour himself was getting cold feet. Then only a few days later our deepest fears are confirmed when we hear him, now hanging on the cross, cry out those famous despairing words, 'My God, my God, why hast thou forsaken me?!'[9]

Why indeed?! The fact is that Jesus only makes these apocalyptic warnings when he is well and truly on the way to his death, and those despairing words I have just quoted are literally his last.[10] Three days later the ordeal is over, by all accounts, he rises from the dead, all is sweetness and light and hope again, the excitement of the job done and the Kingdom now coming, about to burst on a world unsuspecting.

John the Revelator's apocalyptic vision also occurs under duress, the widespread persecution of early Christian believers for their defiance of the Roman cult sometime around the reigns of emperors Nero, Vespasian and Domitian, circa 60–95 CE. John himself was suffering in exile on Patmos for his missionary activities. In his vision cataclysm seems imminent, but of course it did not come and still has not, and two hundred years later the tables were turned under Constantine, as we have seen, the now imperially approved church more persecutor than persecuted. Are we then, as we have suggested, to interpret the dramatic imagery of Revelation—the Seven Seals, the four Horsemen of the Apocalypse, the Seven Trumpets, the Lamb, The Woman, the Dragon, the Two Beasts, the Seven Bowls, the Whore of Babylon— merely as psychological pyrotechnics brought on by the terrible circumstances John and many of the believers found themselves in; or is real and substantial meaning to be found in the affirmation of an inevitable, eventual happy outcome to our human story, regardless of how dire things might look at particular points along the way?

Eventual happy outcome: New Heaven, New Earth, New Jerusalem. You can get a taste of what our apparently assured future might be like at the end of Tolkien's mid-twentieth century fantasy epic, the Lord of the Rings, an amazing psychodrama culminating in a final great battle and the literal return and crowning of a great king. Yes, the trilogy was written against the backdrop of two actual world wars, which might explain all the terrifying deadly violence depicted, the endless, bloody piling up of bodies. But the final ending, if you can momentarily suspend your twenty-first century cynicism,

---

9. Matt 27:46 (KJV).
10. As recorded by Matt and Mk (15:34). Luke has 'Father, into your hands I commit my spirit' (23:46); Jhn, simply, 'It is finished' (19:30).

is a marvellous, joyful affirmation of life, a delicious depiction of the triumph of great good over real evil.

Corny, trite, naïve, just plain silly, to be sure—there, your cynicism has returned! The irony is that most of us in the west now have lived in enduring peace and prosperity, with rapidly rising standards of living, strengthening of democracy and human rights, since Tolkien's time—and that of his great contemporary, CS Lewis, who wrote an equally famous children's version of the final great battle and triumph of good over evil—but we are the ones who are now incapable, as we have noted, of anything but doom and gloom about the future of our species. The essential difference which makes all the difference between them then and us now? A little matter of a God who once existed but apparently no longer does.

We're going over old ground and I'm a cracked record. There is no downplaying of the current threats to humanity, which we rehearsed at the start of this book and have come back to many times; and yes, as I write, Russia seems to be getting the upper hand again in Ukraine, the people of Israel, Gaza and Southern Lebanon are experiencing their own private apocalypse, and Trump has made a famous comeback. But our rejection of the God who does exist—our incapability of even imagining such an unlikely being anymore—not only distorts our perception of the problems we face, it amplifies, ramps them up to end-of-the-world status, and is, as I have claimed, an essential part of the cause of these problems in the first place.

All human problems, as we have repeatedly said, have their origins in common or garden human selfishness, but what we really fear when we descend into despair and imagine the worst for the world is the triumph of something much more potent and dangerous, namely evil—that the power of evil will somehow, in the end, always be stronger than the power of good, that the good guys might not in fact win the great final battle.

As we described it in Chapter 4, in the context of the Garden story, evil is what individual human selfishness becomes when it heads out into the cultural collective and acquires a virtual life of its own, forming deadly features of social, political and economic systems the world over. Well might we fear it, yet at the same time we're fascinated by it and find it hard to resist the temptations it offers. When we give way to it, we plug ourselves into a power source which takes us way beyond our individual limitations, so that individuals and groups do terrible things they would be utterly incapable of doing as solo individuals, participate in systems of oppression that hold people in a stranglehold for decades or even centuries. Just look at the destructive power of cultural evils such as nationalism, racism, authoritarianism, nihilism, sexism, religious fundamentalism, not to mention toxic aspects of colonialism, capitalism and socialism. No one seems to have even gotten around yet to labelling other insidious horrors such as the cultural power that drives pornography, the destructive culture of recreational drug use, or the evil that draws individuals and communities into organized crime. And, in this book, as you have probably noticed, I am adding atheism to this long list of cultural evils, in my view the latest and greatest of them all.

> For we wrestle not against flesh and blood, but against principalities, against powers, against the rulers of the darkness of this world, against spiritual wickedness in high places.[11]

So declares the Apostle Paul, writing circa 60 CE. Sounds great, but there is some obscure, anachronistic language here, and maybe the old King James version is a bit outdated, so here's a more contemporary translation, based on the best scholarship now available:

> For our struggle is not against blood and flesh but against the rulers, against the authorities, against the cosmic powers of this present darkness, against the spiritual forces of evil in the heavenly places.[12]

Yes, it is still saying the same thing: the real struggle we are up against, the real opposition we face, is not merely the natural selfishness inside every human being, but spiritual wickedness or forces which transcend the individual and have a life and power of their own—forces and powers we're well advised not to go up against without serious outside help. Paul may well have had Satan and his cronies in mind, and would that they were truly all we were up against, because any limited individual creature—luridly grinning, perhaps, as we described them in the introduction, with horns, long tail, pitchfork, wings, along with a bunch of similarly gnarly-looking associates—would be a pushover compared to the opposition we really do face!

---

11. Eph 6:12.
12. New Revised Standard Version Updated Edition, 2021.

We delude ourselves, Paul, and I, are saying, if we think it is just a matter of persuasion, education, development, good works by us, even of physical coercion or military force. The transformation of even just one person, from natural selfishness to serious selflessness, is beyond our powers, let alone the transformation of cultural realities, of systems of 'wickedness' which transcend individuals. This goes to the core of the thesis we are presenting in this book: only outside intervention can save us.

Religion, as we saw in Chapter 2, has always been the human attempt to draw down the supernatural powers-that-be—the spirits, gods or God whom we hope will be well-disposed toward us or whom we think we might at least be able to hoodwink into acting in our favour—to combat the powers of darkness that beset us, the devils and demons that seem always eager to possess us and control our behaviour. Paul's insight was, therefore, certainly not original, and belief in the devil, in a great overpowering figure of evil, is as old as the hills, as old at least, for example, as the Genesis story where, as we saw, the serpent plays such a key role.

But the old efforts of religion never quite worked—why? For the reasons we have repeatedly rehearsed. First, the evil in question is always born of the selfish desires of our own hearts, before it takes on a life of its own apart; that is why evil always seems to speak so directly and personally to us, why it always wants to possess us, deep inside. There really is no devil ultimately to blame, therefore, only our natural born selfish selves. Second, we cannot combat this evil born of our selfishness with more selfishness, with more effort of our own to save our own skin, so that being as good as we possibly can, making sacrifices, saying any number of devout prayers, pleading abjectly, buying indulgences, let alone resorting to trickery or deception, won't work, and will almost certainly only compound the evil we are trying to combat in the first place.

There is no solution, in fact, other than faith in and obedience to the invisible God of love, the remarkable deity whom we've begrudgingly rediscovered in this book, despite our best historic efforts to disbelieve them into non-existence. The critical moment, which Paul was picking up on and trying to express as best he could, seems to come, as we have noted, around 1–33 CE, in what is now the Palestinian Territories and the modern state of Israel, with the Jewish Messiah who turns out to be a lot more than that: the invisible God breaks open the whole futile religious enterprise by showing up in person. To the early believers it was simply known as 'the Way', according to some sources: a way of life rather than a formal religious belief and practice, based on faith and trust in the God of love, on letting go of self and selfless consideration and service of one another, friends, strangers, enemies alike, in community and society. Jesus himself spoke continually, as we have seen, of the Kingdom, which he inaugurated through his death and resurrection, a growing, coming state of the world in which this radical way of life would become the rule, not the exception.

Of course, in time the Way became a religion, and organised Christianity has been a very mixed blessing, as we saw in the previous chapters, forcing believers continually back to the source, to rediscover, as we've attempted to do in this book, the God who somehow keeps popping out of existence. Keep going back to the source, the well: St Paul has a strong sense of this in the succeeding verses. To combat the evil cultural forces that constantly surround and threaten us, including religious fundamentalism and its flipside atheism, we need to, constantly, every day, put on the metaphorical 'armour of God'[13]: the 'belt of truth', the 'breastplate of righteousness', the 'sandals of peace', the 'shield of faith', the 'helmet of salvation', the 'sword of the Spirit'. It is a colourful list, the stuff of children's story books and stern sermons. 'Pray in the Spirit at all times in every prayer and supplication', Paul urges. Yes, it is warfare alright, against the twin horrors of natural-born human selfishness and 'the cosmic powers of this present darkness . . . the spiritual forces of evil in the heavenly places'; don't go up against them in your own puny strength, in other words, only with serious divine back-up and weaponry!

Which makes atheism all the more dastardly an evil; and if it was not for the fact that, as we have already seen, rejection of God and the seductive notion that we can do it all better on our own, thank you very much, is the 'original sin' of humanity, as old as our species itself, we'd find it very hard not to suspect that atheism is the devil's, the serpent's, latest and greatest ruse to win us over to his side. This is Putin mocking the west, you stand for nothing, you are divided, you are 'the empire of lies', he sneers, while lying through his teeth, 'we will not invade Ukraine'. 'The fool hath said in his heart, "There is no God"'[14]: we are certainly the fools. 'God does not die', writes Dag Hammarskjold,

---

13. Eph 6:13–20.
14. Ps 14:1 (KJV).

> ... on the day when we cease to believe in a personal deity, but we die on the day when our lives cease to be illuminated by the steady radiance, renewed daily, of a wonder, the source of which is beyond all reason.[15]

Yes, we die on that day, or we are at least dead people walking. We've traced our woes back to primordial times, to Eve and Adam in a walled Garden, to *homo sapiens* emerging out of the fuzzy background of non-self-conscious animalia; and to you and I growing up, nurtured and taught by our loving parents, all the while tempted and torn by the natural self-centredness inside us and the evil potentialities without. All the while, too, the invisible God has been at work—or so it seems we now have to admit, for otherwise there is no way of accounting for the plain fact that our species has managed to survive at all, let alone mostly thrive as it has—at work teaching us the very thing we need in order to survive and thrive, namely the simple capacity to be, from time to time, when the opportunity or need presents itself, selfless.

The incredible events in Israel/Palestine 2000 years ago were, as we've repeatedly said, the culmination of this God's 'plan of salvation', and we are here, now, today, more than 2000 years on from that time (by my calculation), the 'Kingdom of God', inaugurated back then, presumably now well advanced. Yet we find ourselves now in the amazing polycrisis, the perfect apocalyptic storm of social, political, economic and environmental disaster looming, at the same time as most of us in the privileged west have abandoned belief in God. How can we, on our own, rein in the toxic cultural forces that have been unleashed? Clearly, we cannot.

But the seeds of the solution, of hope are definitely here all around us, in this Kingdom of God 2000 years advanced, in the democratic uncertainty and hesitation that the Putins of this world mock, in the culture of human rights and responsibilities that continues to grow around the world. There is, of course, that one critical thing missing: you like me, will need to swallow your pride, admit you're wrong and go back to the source, the divine wellspring of selfless lovingkindness. And, really, I can tell you from experience, it is no chore at all, just sheer delight.

---

15. Dag Hammarskjold, *Markings* [1963], English translation by Leif Sjöberg (London: Faber and Faber, 1964), 64.

Post-script

But still, you are going to want me to confess, once more, to the inexplicable exclusiveness of the event: one time, one place, one people, one religious tradition, to the exclusion of all others. Yes, you understand that what previously had been confined to one 'chosen people', now, with Jesus of Nazareth, becomes universally available; but still there is the troubling, even offensive fact that so many peoples around the world had to wait for centuries before the 'good news' arrived on their shores, and even then it came not as a gift freely offered but with colonial strings attached. Yes, you get that genuine democracy and human rights seem to come into the world exclusively through the Christian tradition, but that does not excuse in any way the colonial destruction of traditional cultures, and in any case you suspect that we in the west have a lot to learn from these cultures, and maybe what we think is good news is not, in the final wash up, all that it's cracked up to be anyway.

Yes, you get that Jesus came to a poor, oppressed, marginalised people, sweating under the iron rule of a murderous empire and their own corrupt rulers, religious and secular. He taught them, fed them, healed them and showed them a radical new way of living; then they (the rulers) murdered him. That certainly is compelling, in anyone's book. But it is the next bit that still you can't come at, his alleged resurrection three days later. Then to compound the impression that it's all just crazy talk, eyewitness accounts written several decades later have him, forty days after the miracle resurrection, slowly rising into the sky and disappearing altogether—although not before promising, as we have seen, to come again one day.

But no, as we noted in Chapter 6, the teachings of Jesus are essentially meaningless if all he did was die a miserable martyr's death; so, the resurrection is no optional extra we can take or leave. Dare to believe it then! It gets worse however: beyond the promised second coming we will supposedly all have our own mini resurrection (Chapter 6 again), a delightful if implausible thought, except that it is only, by all accounts, the believers who will actually get a guernsey on the great day.

Eek, we're back in the counterfeit Gospel, back in gnostic days, in old time religion! But no, this is not an immediate passage to an otherworldly afterlife, like Tutankhamun with all his worldly goods and slaves in tow; or good old Joe, who'll be havin' a beer up there with his mates right now, a heavenly reunion of the deceased members of the pub social club. Rather it's a future resurrection, attendant upon Jesus' second coming, whenever that will be, replete with a brand new "imperishable" body[16], right here on planet earth. It's a crazy, highly speculative, but surprisingly plausible notion, as we also saw in Chapter 6; we get a taste of it every single time we think and act selflessly, when we imaginatively project our consciousness out of our own body, into the body of another person, walk a metre or two in their shoes, see the world through their eyes (as I said back then)—the quintessential out-of-body experience which might just be a figure of the great future day of resurrection to come.

Hmm… through gritted teeth you might now admit its plausibility; but no, no, no, still it is exclusive—not everyone will make the cut on that day—how bigoted, how cruel! Yes, not everyone will undergo the *metanoia* we have repeatedly referred to, the transition from natural-born selfishness to very unnatural selflessness, the little death and rebirth everyday it entails. Not everyone will escape the prison of self, it is true, but God is not the jailer, we are our own jailer if we choose self over selflessness, it is a choice we are making, to condemn ourselves to our own personal, private hell, a hell in the self-centred life we live now, and beyond physical death surely only the oblivion of non-existence, because self-centredness is already oblivion, non-existence. Here is a passage from the marvellous little book, *The Great Divorce* by CS Lewis, which says it all—a conversation between the narrator and an imagined George Macdonald, the famous nineteenth century Presbyterian minister and fantasy writer:

> 'Then those people are right who say that Heaven and Hell are only states of mind?'
>
> 'Hush,' said he [George] sternly. 'Do not blaspheme. Hell is a state of mind—ye never said a truer word. And every state of mind, left to itself, every shutting up of the creature within the dungeon of its own mind—is, in the end, Hell. But Heaven is not a state of mind. Heaven is reality itself. All that is fully real is Heavenly. For all that can be shaken will be shaken and only the unshakeable remains.'[17]

---

16. 1 Cor 15:53 (NIV).
17. C S Lewis, *The Great Divorce* [1946] (UK: Fontana, 1972), 63.

'Heaven is reality itself'—make sure you say it in a broad Scots accent. So, choose the reality of selflessness every day of the week over the unreality, the non-existence, the Hell, of self. Somehow, though apparently localized in space and time, Jesus the Messiah, the Christ, overflows that thirty-three-year incarnation, is the imminence of the invisible God of love in all cultures, all places, all times. Embrace it and live by it; it is (as I've said before) too good not to be true!

Bibliography

Please go to my website, *antitheologia.com*, for essays, articles and reflections on topics relating to the ideas and issues of this book.

Saint Augustine. *Concerning the City of God, against the pagans* [413–427CE], English translation by Henry Bettinson (London: Penguin, 1972).

Saint Augustine. *Confessions* [397–8CE], English translation by RS Pine-Coffin (London: Penguin, 1961).

Bergson, Henri. *Matter and Memory* [1896], English translation by NM Paul and WS Palmer (London: George Allen and Unwin, 1911).

Bergson, Henri. *Creative Evolution* [1907], English translation by Donald A Landes (Oxford: Routledge, 2023).

Bergson, Henri. *The Two Sources of Morality and Religion* [1932], English translation by RA Audra and C Brereton (London: Macmillan, 1935).

Bohm, David. *Wholeness and the Implicate Order* (London: Routledge and Kegan Paul, 1980).

Bonhoeffer, Dietrich, *The Cost of Discipleship* [1937], English translation by RH Fuller (London: SCM Press, 1948).

Bonhoeffer, Dietrich, *A Testament to Freedom*, edited by GB Kelly and FB Nelson (San Fransisco: Harper Collins, 1990).

Borg, Marcus and Crossan, John Dominic, *The Last Week* (San Francisco: Harper One, 2007).

Boulton, David. *The Trouble with God: Religious Humanism and the Republic of Heaven* (UK: John Hunt, 2002).

Boyce, James. *Born Bad: Original Sin and the Making of the Western World* (Melbourne: Black Inc, 2015).

Camus, Albert. *The Rebel* [1951], English translation by Anthony Bower (London: Penguin, 2000).

Darwin, Charles. *On the Origin of Species* [1859], edited by J Carroll (Ontario: Broadview Press, 2003).

Dawkins, Richard. *The Selfish Gene* (UK: Oxford University Press, 1976).

Dewey, John. *The Quest for Certainty* (New York: Minton, Balch, 1929).

Dostoevsky, Fyodor. *Demons* (also known as *The Possessed*, *The Devils*) [1871–1872], English translation by RA Maguire (London: Penguin, 2008).

Drayton, Dean. *Apocalyptic Good News* (Eugene, Oregon: Resource Publications, 2019).

Edwards, Denis. *The God of Evolution* (New York: Paulist Press, 1999).

Endo, Shusaku. *A Life of Jesus* [1973], English translation by RA Schuchert (New Jersey: Paulist Press, 1978).

Endo, Shusaku. *Silence* [1966], English translation by William Johnston (USA: Picador, 2016).

Henrich, Joseph. *The Weirdest People in the World*, Penguin, 2020.

Holland, Tom. *Dominion* (London: Little, Brown, 2019).

Jung, CG. *Modern Man in Search of a Soul* (London: Kegan Paul, 1933).

Kazantzakis, Nikos. *The Last Temptation of the Christ* [1952], English translation by PA Bien (New York: Simon & Schuster, 1960).

Kierkegaard, Søren. *The Sickness unto Death* [1849], English translation by Alastair Hannay (London: Penguin, 1989).

Lefebvre, Alexandre. *Human Rights as a Way of* Life (Stanford: Stanford University Press, 2013).

Lewis, CS. *The Four Loves* [1960] (London: William Collins, 2012).

Lewis, CS. *The Great Divorce* [1946] (UK: Fontana, 1972).

Pals, Daniel L. *Seven Theories of Religion* (UK: Oxford University Press, 1996).

Pearson, Keith Ansell. *Philosophy and the Adventure of the Virtual* (London: Routledge, 2002).

Rainbow Spirit Elders. *Rainbow Spirit Theology: Towards an Australian Aboriginal Theology*, Second Edition (Adelaide: ATF Press, 2007).

Scruton, Roger. *The Soul of the World* (USA: Princeton University Press, 2014).

Solzhenitsyn, Alexander. *The Gulag Archipelago* [1973], English translation by TP Whitney and H Willets (London: Harvill, 1986).

Wenham, G J. *World Biblical Commentary,* Volume 1, Genesis 1–15 (Texas: Word Books, 1987).

Wilson, A N. *God's Funeral* (London: Abacus, 2000).

Wilson, Derek. *Out of the Storm: The Life and Legacy of Martin Luther* (London: Pimlico, 2008).

Wolters, Albert M. *Creation Regained: Biblical Basics for a Reformational World-view* (Grand Rapids: Eardmans, 1985).

www.ingramcontent.com/pod-product-compliance
Ingram Content Group UK Ltd.
Pitfield, Milton Keynes, MK11 3LW, UK
UKHW010326280625
460175UK00004B/21